BEACH BLISS

A Guide for Recharging Your Life on Your Beach Vacation

Beach Bliss: A Guide for Recharging Your Life on Your Beach Vacation

By: Caroline Ruth Bailey

Copyright © 2025
Caroline Ruth Bailey All rights reserved

No part of this publication may be reproduced, distributed, or transmitted in any form or by any means, including photocopying, recording, or other electronic or mechanical methods, without the prior written permission of the publisher, except as permitted by U.S. copyright law. For permission requests, contact the Author at Caroline Bailey, PO Box 941 Supply, NC 28462 or at carolinebaileync@gmail.com

This publication is designed to provide accurate and authoritative information in regard to the subject matter covered. It is sold with the understanding that neither the author nor the publisher is engaged in rendering legal, investment, accounting or other professional services. While the publisher and author have used their best efforts in preparing this book, they make no representations or warranties with respect to the accuracy or completeness of the contents of this book and specifically disclaim any implied warranties of merchantability or fitness for a particular purpose. No warranty may be created or extended by sales representatives or written sales materials. The advice and strategies contained herein may not be suitable for your situation. You should consult with a professional when appropriate. Neither the publisher nor the author shall be liable for any loss of profit or any other commercial damages, including but not limited to special, incidental, consequential, personal, or other damages.

This book is dedicated to Noel.

Tiny Tiger of Holden Beach,
Magic Beach Cat of my heart.

Contents

Using your 6 days at the Beach for a Mental and Emotional Reset..............vi

Day 1 ~ On Beach Time: Settling In and Disconnecting 1

Day 2 ~ Shifting Sands: Releasing What You Can't Control.......................41

Day 3 ~ Imcoming Swells: High Tides of Renewal 73

Day 4 ~ Waves of Joy: Reconnecting with Nature and Creativity 115

Day 5 ~ Sands of Stillness: Resting and Reconnecting with Gratitiude ...151

Day 6 ~ Bon Voyage: Sailing Home with Purpose 173

Conclusion ~ A Fond Farewell 199

Using your 6 days at the Beach for a Mental and Emotional Reset

In the hustle and bustle of everyday life, it's easy to become overwhelmed by stress, responsibilities, and constant noise. Often, we find ourselves caught up in a whirlwind of tasks, deadlines, and expectations, leaving little time for rest and reflection. A beach vacation, however, offers a perfect opportunity to hit the reset button on our mental and emotional well-being. The soothing sounds of crashing waves, the feel of warm sand beneath our feet, and the rhythmic ebb and flow of the tide provide an ideal environment for releasing stress and reconnecting with ourselves.

The power of nature in restoring balance cannot be overstated. Beaches, with their wide-open spaces and natural beauty, invite us to slow down and take a deep breath. The simplicity of the environment helps quiet the constant chatter of our minds. As we step away from our everyday routines, the beach creates a sense of spaciousness, allowing our thoughts to settle and our emotions to recalibrate. In a world where we are constantly multitasking and juggling priorities, the beach serves as a sanctuary, offering a much-needed break from the overstimulation of modern life.

The beach provides a unique opportunity for introspection. Whether it's taking a solo walk along the shoreline, reading a book under the shade of an umbrella, or simply watching the sunset, the beach encourages mindfulness. This form of meditation in motion allows us to observe our thoughts and feelings without judgment. We can reflect on our lives, reassess our priorities, and gain clarity on decisions that may have seemed clouded by stress or uncertainty. In this way, the beach acts as a natural space for emotional cleansing and mental renewal.

In addition to being a space for reflection, the beach offers a chance for relaxation and rejuvenation. The combination of physical relaxation and mental stillness creates a harmonious environment where both mind and body can heal. The natural beauty of the ocean, the salty air, and the sunshine all have therapeutic effects, promoting relaxation, reducing anxiety, and enhancing mood. Taking time to simply be present and immerse oneself in the serenity of the beach provides the emotional reset many of us need to return to our lives feeling refreshed and revitalized.

A beach vacation serves as more than just a getaway; it is an opportunity for transformation. By stepping away from the chaos of everyday life and immersing ourselves in the tranquility of the beach, we give ourselves the space to heal and recharge. This break not only helps alleviate stress but also fosters a deeper connection to ourselves and our inner peace. As we return from the beach, we are better equipped to face challenges with renewed perspective, emotional resilience, and a clearer sense of purpose.

Why I Wrote This Book

The beach has always held a special place in my heart. Growing up, my family would camp on the west end of Holden Beach, where the sand dunes met the sky, and life seemed to slow down. Even as an adult, I found myself returning to this stretch of shore whenever I needed to reset, recharge, or simply breathe. The beach has always been more than just a destination for me—it's been a place of healing and transformation.

Like many of you, I know what it feels like to be caught up in the whirlwind of life, where work, responsibilities, and endless to-do lists leave little room for rest. Over the years, I've discovered that the ocean has a way of bringing us back to ourselves. Its rhythms remind us to slow down, its vastness invites us to dream, and its beauty encourages us to find joy in the present moment.

But this isn't about my story—it's about yours. Whether this is your first visit to the beach or a cherished tradition, the time you spend here is an opportunity to reconnect with what matters most. This book is a guide to help you savor those moments, carry the peace of the shore with you, and find ways to weave that calm into your everyday life.

As you read through these pages, my hope is that you'll feel inspired to create your own rituals of rest and renewal. Whether it's through simple mindfulness practices, journaling prompts, or quiet moments of reflection, I want you to discover the tools that work for you.

The ocean has taught me that every wave brings a fresh start. As you begin this journey, I hope you'll embrace the wisdom of the shore, take what you need from this experience, and carry a piece of the beach home with you—wherever that may be.

How the 6-Day Structure Will Help Maximize Your Vacation

When you embark on a beach vacation, the goal isn't just to escape, but to truly reset—mentally, emotionally, and physically. The 6-day structure I've designed for you is intended to make the most of every moment, ensuring that each day offers something purposeful and transformative. It's not about rushing through your time at the beach; it's about immersing yourself fully in each day and embracing the experience with intention.

The first day of your 6-day reset is all about arriving and disconnecting from the outside world. It's natural to feel the weight of everyday life as you step away, so this first day is dedicated to grounding yourself in the present moment. Unpack slowly, breathe deeply, and get familiar with the rhythm of the ocean. Take some time to explore the beach, dip your toes in the water, and let go of the tension from your travels. This is the start of your reset—by giving yourself permission to let go of obligations and distractions, you make space for the healing and reflection that's to come.

Days 2 through 4 are about embracing the transformative power of nature. This is when you'll be diving deeper into activities that help you connect with yourself, the environment, and the healing energy of the beach. Whether it's early morning walks along the shore, journaling at sunrise, or engaging in mindful breathing while watching the waves, these days are about reconnecting with the present. The ocean will become your therapist, the breeze your guide, and the rhythm of the tides your reminder that life, too, moves through cycles of calm and change. These activities are designed to help you break free from the constant hustle and bustle and focus on what truly matters—your mental and emotional well-being.

By day 5, you'll have a deeper sense of clarity. It's time to reflect on the healing that's taken place, but also to start setting intentions for your return to everyday life. It's about taking all that you've learned and experienced so far and creating actionable steps to carry that peace and insight into your regular routine. In these final days, you'll focus on recharging and nurturing the areas of your life that need attention. Take some time to journal, make a plan, and set your intentions for moving forward—whether it's a healthier mindset, a more intentional routine, or a renewed sense of self.

Finally, day 6 is your return to yourself. This day is about integration and closure—taking the lessons from the week and incorporating them into your life. Before you leave, spend time reflecting on how far you've come in just six days. Revisit your favorite moments from the week, whether it was a conversation with a stranger, a quiet moment on the beach, or an epiphany you had while watching the waves. This is where you can look back and see the transformation you've undergone, knowing you can carry that peace with you as you return to your everyday life.

The beauty of this 6-day structure is that it's not just about a vacation; it's about making the most of every moment to heal, reset, and recharge. By breaking your time into these intentional stages, you can maximize your experience and leave with not just memories of the beach, but with a new sense of clarity and purpose. When you step away from the chaos of life and immerse yourself in nature, you're not just recharging your body; you're giving your mind and heart the space to heal and evolve. By the time you head back home, you'll be ready to face life's challenges with a renewed sense of strength and peace.

Day 1 ~

On Beach Time:

Settling In and

Disconnecting from the Rush

New Beginnings:

The Transformative Power of Arrival

The concept of arrival marks a pivotal moment in any journey, especially when we transition from the hectic rhythm of everyday life to the calming presence of the beach. Upon arriving, we are not just stepping into a new physical space; we are stepping into a mental and emotional space that allows for peace and rest.

In our fast-paced world, we rarely take the time to truly "arrive." Our minds are often distracted, still thinking about the tasks we left behind or the work awaiting us when we return. But to fully embrace the power of arrival, we must intentionally focus on the present moment and leave behind all the clutter of daily life. The beach, with its vast openness and calming energy, is the perfect place to begin this process.

To truly arrive is to shift our mindset, to be present and open to what the environment has to offer. This moment requires us to pause, take a deep breath, and recognize the change in both our surroundings and our internal state.

When we arrive at the beach, we experience a physical and emotional shift. The sight of the waves, the feel of the sand underfoot, and the sound of the water immediately pull us into the present. For many, this feeling of arrival signifies a break from the responsibilities and expectations that often feel overwhelming. It's a moment where the body and mind can reconnect, grounding us in the present and creating space for renewal.

The process of arrival also involves letting go of the mental baggage we carry. It's easy to be caught up in the stressors of life, whether they are work-related, personal, or otherwise. But as we arrive at the beach, we have the opportunity to consciously leave these stressors behind.

This isn't about ignoring problems, but about recognizing that the beach, in all its tranquility, offers us the space we need to reset. The act of "arriving" invites us to mentally unpack as we physically do the same, giving ourselves permission to leave behind worries and simply exist in the moment.

Arrival also represents an emotional release, allowing us to reconnect with ourselves. The busy pace of life often means we neglect our emotional needs, prioritizing external demands over internal well-being. Yet, upon arrival at the beach, we are given the opportunity to check in with ourselves emotionally.

We can ask, "What do I need right now?" or "How do I feel?" By embracing the moment of arrival, we take our first step in rediscovering emotional balance and healing. This sense of arrival is not just about changing locations but about recalibrating our emotional state and embracing a fresh perspective.

Ultimately, the act of arriving at the beach symbolizes a transition from the demands of daily life to a space of peace, relaxation, and healing. This shift is critical in setting the tone for the vacation experience. By consciously allowing ourselves to arrive, we set the stage for a more meaningful, rejuvenating time at the beach, one that will foster a deeper connection to both ourselves and the environment around us. The concept of arrival is not just about physical presence; it's about engaging with the place and with ourselves in a way that promotes true relaxation and renewal.

Unwinding with the Tides:

Living at the Beach's Tempo

Once we've arrived, the next step is to embrace the slower pace of the beach. In a world that constantly urges us to keep moving faster, the beach offers us a rare opportunity to slow down. The waves that gently roll onto the shore set the rhythm for this experience, encouraging us to adopt a more deliberate pace.

There's no rush when you're at the beach; it's a place where time seems to stretch, allowing us to appreciate the present moment without the pressure of doing anything at all. This slower pace becomes the perfect antidote to the hustle and bustle of everyday life, providing us the freedom to just be.

Slowing down at the beach isn't just about physical relaxation; it's about embracing a mental shift. In our everyday routines, we are often conditioned to focus on the next task, the next goal, or the next deadline. But the slower pace of the beach invites us to let go of these pressures.

As we walk along the shoreline or sit quietly by the water, we can tune into the rhythm of the waves, which operate without urgency. By allowing ourselves to synchronize with this natural pace, we begin to release the need for constant movement and productivity. In doing so, we create space for mindfulness, allowing us to engage more fully in the experience of being at the beach.

The slower pace is also a reminder that it's okay to take a break. Many people find it difficult to stop and rest, often feeling guilty about the time they spend doing nothing. However, the beach teaches us that rest is necessary for renewal.

The act of slowing down at the beach allows our minds and bodies to recharge. Whether it's sitting in a beach chair, taking a slow stroll along the shore, or simply lying in the sand, the beach encourages us to embrace the gift of rest. This slower pace allows us to reconnect with our own rhythms and reminds us that our well-being doesn't depend on how much we accomplish, but on how well we care for ourselves.

Letting go of immediate pressures and expectations is a key aspect of slowing down. When we arrive at the beach, we have the opportunity to release the burdens of our everyday lives. There's no need to check emails or worry about deadlines; instead, we can immerse ourselves fully in the present.

By relinquishing these pressures, we free ourselves from the mental clutter that often accompanies daily life. This gives us the space to relax and recalibrate, allowing us to return to our routines feeling refreshed and renewed. The slower pace of the beach is a perfect backdrop for this process, as it nurtures our ability to let go of stress and simply be.

As we embrace the slower pace of the beach, we invite a greater sense of peace and tranquility into our lives. The beach becomes a sanctuary for mindfulness, where the natural world encourages us to focus on the present and let go of distractions.

By slowing down, we allow ourselves to be more attuned to the sights, sounds, and sensations around us. The beach, in its infinite stillness, teaches us that there is power in slowing down. As we take time to unwind, reflect, and be still, we create a foundation for a deeper emotional and mental reset, one that will extend far beyond the beach.

Disconnecting from the Grind:

Shifting Your Focus from Work

Naming the Strain:

Recognizing What's Behind Your Stress

One of the first steps in mentally "checking out" is recognizing what's been weighing you down. Whether it's work, obligations, or expectations from others, our stressors often occupy space in our minds without us even realizing it.

These mental burdens can make it difficult to truly relax and be present, especially when we're stepping away from the demands of everyday life. By taking a moment to identify what's causing us stress, we begin to release its grip on us.

Acknowledging the things that have been crowding our minds helps to create the mental space necessary for rest and rejuvenation. When we acknowledge what's on our minds, we also create the opportunity to let go of those thoughts. We no longer have to carry that mental clutter. By simply writing down or mentally noting the things that are causing stress—be it a looming project, unresolved tasks, or nagging worries—we are taking the first step toward release.

This act of recognition creates distance between us and our stress, offering the space needed to embrace the present moment. When we do this, we shift the focus away from what we need to do, to what we need to let go of.

Often, it's easy to forget how much mental energy we spend holding on to stress, even when we're on vacation. Whether it's worries about the future, concerns about unfinished tasks, or expectations of ourselves, these stressors can follow us if we don't intentionally address them.

By identifying and naming them, we put ourselves in a position to release that burden. This process is freeing because it allows us to move away from the mental weight that prevents us from enjoying our time at the beach.

When we engage in this practice of recognizing and naming our stress, we are also giving ourselves permission to let it go. It's a way of saying, "This no longer serves me; I am ready to step away from it." This simple act of mental decluttering is the first step toward reclaiming our peace.

The beach, with its calming atmosphere, serves as the perfect contrast to our daily worries. The waves crashing on the shore are a reminder that stress is like the tides—sometimes it's overwhelming, but it will pass.

By identifying our stressors, we can begin to disengage from them, allowing ourselves the space we need to relax. This step is essential in the process of resetting our minds and embracing the calm that the beach offers. Recognizing what's weighing on us and intentionally choosing to leave it behind is the first step toward truly enjoying this reset.

From Rush to Relaxation: Navigating the Transition to Calm

Arriving at the beach isn't just a physical change of location; it's an opportunity to mentally reset. Day 1 offers a unique chance to transition from the hustle and bustle of daily life into the slower pace of the beach. This shift in mindset is crucial for making the most of your time away.

Think of this day as a mental "reset"—a deliberate pause in your usual routine to allow your mind to unwind and prepare for the calm that follows. It's the moment to say goodbye to the demands of work and to fully embrace the slower pace of life that awaits.

The key to this transition is recognizing that you don't have to immediately jump into vacation mode; you can ease into it. Give yourself permission to let go of the "to-do" list, the endless emails, or the mental checklist of tasks that follow you. Allow yourself to be in the moment.

The beach, with its peaceful environment, invites you to shift gears, but it requires you to mentally release the hold that work and obligations have on you. This is the time to slow down, to breathe, and to be present.

This transition also involves letting go of the need to be productive. Often, when we take time off, there's a subtle pressure to "make the most of it"—to fill our days with activities, exploration, or achievements. But the beauty of the beach is that it allows you to step away from this mindset.

The natural pace of the waves reminds us that sometimes, simply existing in a space is enough. This first day is about creating mental space, where the focus shifts away from being productive and towards being present and grounded.

It's important to recognize that this transition is a process, not an instant change. Don't rush it. Give yourself the grace to step away from the pressures of daily life at your own pace. The transition into vacation mode should feel like a gentle flow, not a forced jump.

As the day unfolds, allow yourself to be fully immersed in the sensory experience of the beach—the sound of the waves, the feel of the sand, the scent of the ocean breeze. These simple sensations will help guide you into the relaxed state you seek.

By the time the sun sets on your first day, you should feel the shift. This is the power of a mental reset. By intentionally allowing yourself to transition out of work mode and into vacation mode, you lay the groundwork for the reset ahead. This is the first and most important step toward a more peaceful, relaxed state of mind for the rest of your time at the beach.

Mindful Beginnings:

Setting the Tone for a Meaningful Week

Setting intentions for your time at the beach helps to shape how you experience this reset. Intentions are not rigid goals; rather, they are guiding principles that help focus your energy in a way that serves your well-being.

On Day 1, take a moment to reflect on what you want to release and what you want to bring into your week. Setting these intentions is about focusing on what you need during this time—whether it's rest, self-reflection, or simply taking time to breathe deeply and let go.

Your intentions for the week will provide clarity on what you hope to achieve mentally, emotionally, or physically. Maybe your intention is to slow down and be present, letting go of any expectations that you have to be busy or productive. Maybe you want to prioritize self-care—taking long walks, journaling by the shore, or simply spending time in quiet solitude.

Whatever your intentions are, be clear about what you want to focus on and what you want to leave behind. This sense of direction helps to align your energy with what truly matters during your time away.

Setting clear intentions also gives you permission to let go of outside pressures. When we step away from work or other obligations, we often carry the weight of expectations with us. Setting an intention to focus on your own well-being helps to remove that pressure.

It's an opportunity to free yourself from the mental burdens that you've been carrying, allowing you to fully immerse in the experience of relaxation. By letting go of what's weighing you down, you create space for growth, clarity, and peace.

Your intentions also help to create a purposeful vacation, where you are actively engaging in your own restoration. The beach offers a natural environment to reflect and reset, and by setting intentions, you give yourself a framework to work within.

This is not about achieving specific tasks but about being present and intentional with your time. The process of setting intentions is like planting seeds for personal growth. It's about identifying the things that need attention—whether it's rest, self-compassion, or clarity—and nurturing them throughout the week.

By the end of your stay, you will likely look back and realize how powerful your intentions were in shaping your experience. Setting them on the first day helps you stay connected to the core purpose of your time at the beach: to reset, to rest, and to reconnect with yourself.

Whether your intention was to rest deeply or gain clarity on something that's been troubling you, you'll return from your trip feeling refreshed and aligned with your goals. Setting intentions creates a roadmap for a truly meaningful and restorative vacation.

Unwind and Settle:

A Calming Routine for Your Arrival

From Suitcase to Serenity: The Art of Intentional Unpacking

Unpacking may seem like a mundane task, but when approached with intention, it can be the first step in setting the tone for your entire stay. Instead of rushing through it, take your time. As you open your suitcase, think of each item as part of a process that's helping you settle into the space both physically and mentally. Unfold your clothes slowly, lay out your toiletries with care, and consider the things that bring you comfort.

This process allows you to become fully present in your environment, shifting your focus away from the stressors you left behind. By unpacking intentionally, you begin to create a space that is not just functional but also one that invites relaxation.

As you unpack, consider the idea of "creating space" not just for your belongings but for your well-being. The act of setting down your items can be a symbolic gesture of releasing the mental clutter you've been carrying. By taking time to arrange things thoughtfully, you are signaling to your mind and body that this is a time for relaxation and rest.

There's no rush—allow the act of unpacking to be meditative. As you go through your things, notice how each item contributes to your sense of comfort and peace, from your favorite pajamas to the cozy throw blanket you can't live without.

Consider unpacking in a way that encourages a sense of order and calm. Since you're staying for several days, take a moment to organize your personal space in a way that reflects what you need for the week. Maybe that means setting up your bathroom counter with your favorite skincare products, or arranging your bedroom so it's peaceful and uncluttered.

This step gives you control over your environment and reinforces the idea that you are choosing a slower, more intentional pace for this time away. Let your surroundings match the internal state you're working toward—one of rest and ease.

Unpacking is also about preparing for the moments of solitude and reflection that are to come. It's easy to feel overwhelmed when we dive straight into vacation mode, but by taking the time to set up your space thoughtfully, you ensure that the energy around you is in alignment with the peacefulness you seek.

Whether you're placing your clothes in the closet or choosing the perfect spot for your book or journal, each small decision is an opportunity to reinforce the calming intentions of your stay. This is your chance to carve out a space that invites you to let go of the rush and embrace the present.

Remember that unpacking with intention isn't about perfection—it's about presence. As you set up your space, avoid feeling pressured to have everything in its "right" place or to be fully organized. The goal is to make your environment feel like a sanctuary where you can unwind and relax.

By slowing down and savoring the process of unpacking, you invite yourself into a more mindful approach to your vacation—one where every moment can be enjoyed and every decision made thoughtfully.

Claiming Your Space:

Crafting Comfort in Your Beach Getaway

Once you've unpacked, it's time to create a space that enhances your sense of calm and invites reflection. Whether it's your bedroom, living area, or even a cozy corner of the balcony, this space should be designed to help you relax and reconnect with yourself.

Start by arranging personal items that bring you comfort—perhaps a favorite book, a journal, or a photograph that holds meaning. These small elements remind you of who you are outside of the roles and responsibilities you've left behind. By surrounding yourself with familiar objects, you help create a space that feels like home, even if you're away from it.

To enhance this space, consider adding soothing sensory elements that engage all of your senses. For example, you might light a candle with a calming scent, or diffuse essential oils that promote relaxation, such as lavender or chamomile. The sense of smell is particularly powerful in influencing our mood, so this small step can immediately shift the atmosphere in your space.

Even something as simple as a vase of fresh flowers can introduce a natural element that feels both refreshing and grounding. The goal is to create a multi-sensory environment that invites you to breathe deeply and let go of any lingering tension.

Another aspect of setting up a calming space is making sure it's free from distractions. If you're staying in a rental or a hotel, you might need to adjust the lighting, or perhaps even rearrange a few things to make the area feel more peaceful. This is your time to reclaim control of your environment.

Make the space your own, even if just for the week, so that it feels like a personal retreat. Consider adding a cozy throw blanket to your bed or setting up a chair where you can sit and meditate or journal. These little touches help to establish a physical space that mirrors the mental space you're working toward.

This space doesn't have to be large or elaborate—it simply needs to reflect your personal sense of peace. Think of it as a small sanctuary that nurtures your body and mind. A calming environment invites you to unwind more deeply, allowing you to be present in the moment and relax into the slower pace of beach life.

Whether it's a corner of your room or a spot by the window, a peaceful area can become your anchor for the rest of the week. It's where you can retreat when the world feels overwhelming and you need a break.

As you settle into your calming space, remember that this ritual is about intentionally creating an environment that supports your reset. When we design spaces that foster peace and comfort, we are setting ourselves up for a deeper connection with the present moment.

This space is yours to fill with the things that bring you peace—whether that's a favorite book, a quiet spot for reflection, or simply the space to breathe and be. It's about cultivating a sanctuary where you can truly relax and let go of the pressures that once seemed so urgent.

Stepping into Serenity:

Your First Moments by the Sea

One of the most grounding and essential rituals of your first day is the "first walk" on the beach. This simple act of walking along the shoreline serves as a powerful signal to your body and mind that your journey has officially begun.

Feel the sand beneath your feet, the warmth of the earth beneath your toes, and the refreshing coolness of the ocean breeze on your skin. This walk allows you to transition from the fast-paced world you left behind into the slower, more present state of mind you seek. The rhythm of the waves and the feeling of the sand help to anchor you in the present moment, grounding your energy and preparing you for the reset ahead.

Taking a first walk on the beach is also a symbolic gesture. As you step onto the sand, you are physically and emotionally stepping away from your old routine and embracing something new. The beach, with its vast horizon and infinite expanse of water, serves as a reminder that there's a world beyond your responsibilities and worries.

This walk represents a mental shift, signaling to your mind that the next several days are about healing, relaxation, and renewal. Allow the sound of the waves to wash away any lingering thoughts from your daily life, making room for peace and clarity.

The walk also invites mindfulness—an opportunity to be fully present in your body and surroundings. As you take each step, focus on the sensations of your feet sinking into the sand, the soft breeze on your face, and the sounds of nature surrounding you. Let go of any distractions and focus solely on the experience of being in nature.

The beauty of the beach, with its vastness and tranquility, helps to quiet the mind and bring attention to the present moment. This walk is an invitation to simply "be"—no expectations, no pressures—just you and the peaceful surroundings.

This walk doesn't need to be long or strenuous—it's about the intention behind it. Whether you walk for ten minutes or an hour, the key is to allow the experience to be a transition point. This ritual signals the beginning of your reset, helping you shift your mindset and begin the process of letting go.

The beach offers a sense of spaciousness, and as you walk, you'll begin to feel that spaciousness expand within you. This ritual is your moment of arrival, where the busy world is left behind and you step into the present moment.

Remember that the first walk on the beach isn't just about taking in the scenery—it's about taking a deep breath and grounding yourself in the stillness of the environment. The beach has a natural way of inviting relaxation, and as you walk along the shore, you're reconnecting with the simple joy of movement and the peace of the ocean.

This ritual serves as an anchor, helping you feel both rooted and free. It marks the official beginning of your vacation reset, reminding you that this is your time to heal, reflect, and reconnect.

The Beauty of Not Knowing:

Thriving in Uncertainty

Uncertainty is one of the few things in life that we can be absolutely certain about. From the moment we wake up each day to the moment we fall asleep, the world around us is full of unknowns. Despite our best efforts to plan and control every aspect of our lives, there are simply too many variables to predict with certainty. The weather, the people we encounter, even our own emotions change unexpectedly.

Uncertainty, therefore, is not something that can be avoided or controlled; it is part of the natural fabric of life. The first step in this reset journey is to acknowledge uncertainty as an inevitable companion. Rather than fearing it, we can begin to accept it, making space for peace and calm.

The goal is not to fight against uncertainty, but to shift our mindset and see it as an opportunity for growth. By embracing the unknown, we allow ourselves the freedom to move forward without the burden of needing everything to be certain.

Much of our modern lives revolve around the pursuit of control. We try to manage our schedules, plan for the future, and structure our lives in ways that minimize unpredictability. However, life has a way of reminding us that we are not the ultimate masters of every outcome.

This conflict between our desire for control and the reality of life's unpredictability can create immense stress. We may find ourselves trying to hold onto control over the smallest of details, only to be confronted with the inevitable—things don't always go as planned.

Part of the reset process is coming to terms with this paradox: recognizing that while we can influence many aspects of our lives, we cannot control everything. Accepting that we cannot control every situation or outcome frees us from the anxiety of needing to "get everything right." This mindset shift allows us to release the pressure of trying to perfect every moment, and instead, embrace life as it comes.

When we acknowledge that uncertainty is part of life, we begin to experience the freedom that comes with letting go of the need for control. The more we cling to rigid plans and expectations, the more we set ourselves up for disappointment and frustration when things inevitably go awry.

On the other hand, when we allow ourselves to embrace uncertainty, we are better able to adapt to the ebb and flow of life. Life, much like the ocean, has its ups and downs, its calm moments and its stormy ones. Just as the waves rise and fall with natural rhythm, so do our challenges and triumphs.

By letting go of the need to control everything, we gain the freedom to focus on what truly matters: living in the moment, accepting what comes, and making the most of it. Uncertainty, when embraced, becomes a powerful force of release, allowing us to be more present and responsive to whatever life presents.

In truth, uncertainty is not a barrier, but a path to growth. It's easy to see the unknown as something to be feared or avoided, but it can actually be a catalyst for personal growth. Every moment of uncertainty invites us to stretch our emotional and mental capacity, forcing us to become more resilient and creative in our responses. When things don't go as planned, we're pushed to adapt, to think differently, and to approach problems from fresh angles.

This is where true growth happens—outside of our comfort zones, in the space where the unexpected occurs. Instead of resisting the unknown, we can begin to see it as a teacher, guiding us toward greater self-awareness and personal strength. The moments of challenge that uncertainty brings are the very moments that can propel us to become stronger versions of ourselves.

Ultimately, the reset process is about living in the present moment, free from the burdens of future worries and past regrets. Uncertainty, when embraced, becomes a bridge to the present. Instead of looking ahead with anxiety or dwelling on what we can't change, we learn to focus on the here and now.

We can begin to notice the small details—the feel of the sand beneath our feet, the sound of the waves crashing on the shore, the fresh air filling our lungs. When we stop trying to control everything, we can experience life more fully, without distraction.

This shift in perspective allows us to be more present with the simple joys of life, and when we allow ourselves to accept and let go of uncertainty, we free ourselves from the constant need to predict and control. By embracing uncertainty, we learn to truly live in the moment, appreciating what is, rather than what we wish it to be.

Tides of Life:

The Ocean's Wisdom for Personal Growth

The ocean is a powerful and timeless symbol that has been used throughout history to represent life's many complexities. Just as the ocean's waves ebb and flow, so too do the challenges we face in our lives. At times, the waves are gentle, rolling softly against the shore, bringing a sense of peace and calm. In these moments, life feels manageable, and the difficulties we encounter seem small in comparison to the vastness of the world around us.

Similarly, there are periods when life flows smoothly, and we feel in harmony with our surroundings, able to manage whatever comes our way with ease. These calm waves reflect the more peaceful times in our lives when we feel in control and at peace with the world.

However, the ocean is not always calm. Sometimes, the waves grow higher, crashing violently against the shore, much like the storms we face in our own lives. These turbulent moments are inevitable and often come when we least expect them. Just as the ocean can suddenly shift from tranquility to turmoil, our lives can take unexpected turns that feel overwhelming.

During these challenging times, it can be easy to feel as though we are drowning in our emotions, caught in the chaos with no way out. But just as the ocean's waves eventually recede, so too do the intense challenges in our lives. While the stormy moments may feel relentless, they always pass, leaving behind a sense of calm and an opportunity to reflect on what we've learned.

The ebb and flow of the ocean also symbolize the cyclical nature of life's challenges. No matter how big or small, obstacles and difficulties will always come and go, just as the tide moves in and out. Understanding this cyclical rhythm can help us navigate difficult moments with a sense of perspective.

We know that, just as the ocean's waves inevitably recede, the challenges we face will eventually subside, making room for new opportunities and growth. Life is not a series of constant waves crashing against us, but a dance between moments of calm and moments of intensity. By embracing this rhythm, we can move through life's challenges with greater resilience, knowing that everything is temporary.

The ocean teaches us the importance of patience and acceptance. We cannot force the waves to calm or make the tide change, just as we cannot control the challenges that arise in our lives. Instead, we must accept them as part of the natural flow of life, knowing that everything has its time and place.

When we resist the ebb and flow of life, we only create more struggle for ourselves. But when we accept that challenges are as much a part of life as moments of peace, we are better equipped to handle whatever comes our way. Just as the ocean moves in its own time, so too do our struggles and triumphs, each playing a role in shaping who we are and how we grow.

In the end, the ocean serves as a reminder that life is constantly changing, and that change is neither inherently good nor bad—it simply is. The waves may crash against the shore, but they also provide the necessary energy for the ecosystem to thrive. Similarly, the challenges we face in life often provide the impetus for growth and transformation.

Just as we cannot control the ocean's rhythm, we must learn to work with life's ebb and flow, accepting both the calm and the storm. By embracing this metaphor, we can learn to navigate our own lives with greater grace, understanding that, like the ocean, life moves in cycles, and each moment is part of a larger, ever-changing process.

In Tune with the Tides:

Seeing Struggles as Part of the Journey

Life, much like the natural world around us, operates in cycles and rhythms that we cannot always predict or control. Just as the seasons shift from spring to summer, fall to winter, so too do the experiences, challenges, and struggles we face in our own personal lives.

The idea that everything has a rhythm—a natural ebb and flow—can be both comforting and liberating. It reminds us that nothing lasts forever, whether it's the tranquility of good times or the turbulence of hard moments. By recognizing and embracing this truth, we can approach our personal struggles with a sense of patience and understanding, knowing that they, too, will pass in their own time.

Personal struggles, much like the changing of the seasons, often come with a natural rhythm. Some days feel heavy and overwhelming, as if the weight of the world is upon us. Other days, we may feel lighter and more at ease, as if we can breathe again and move forward with purpose. This rhythm is not something to fight against, but something to flow with.

Just as nature has its seasons of growth and dormancy, so too do we have periods of challenge and renewal. Accepting that our struggles are temporary and that they will eventually give way to brighter days allows us to move through tough times with greater resilience, rather than feeling hopeless in the face of adversity.

When we embrace the rhythm of personal struggles, we also begin to understand the importance of timing. Just as a storm will eventually clear, we must remind ourselves that our own difficult moments are part of a greater process of growth and change. It may not always be easy to accept the presence of struggle, but by acknowledging that life moves in waves, we can better manage our emotions and expectations.

By embracing the flow, we can find peace even in the midst of turbulence. Knowing that every challenge we face is a step toward personal growth and transformation allows us to move through the pain with purpose, trusting that what we learn along the way will shape us into something stronger.

Additionally, the rhythm of struggle helps us develop a deeper sense of empathy and understanding for ourselves and others. When we see that everyone's life moves in cycles, we can be less judgmental and more compassionate, recognizing that each person's rhythm may differ from our own.

By embracing our own personal struggles as part of the flow of life, we also give ourselves permission to be imperfect and to allow ourselves the space to heal. We don't need to force ourselves out of difficult times; instead, we can trust that the rhythm will shift and that the pain will eventually fade, just as the seasons change from cold to warm.

Ultimately, embracing the idea that everything, including our personal struggles, has a rhythm and a flow brings us peace in the face of adversity. It encourages us to relinquish control and instead trust the process, allowing ourselves to grow with the flow of life.

When we accept that challenges are part of the natural rhythm, we can approach them with a sense of calm, knowing that they will pass in time and that we will emerge from them stronger and wiser. By learning to flow with life's natural cycles, we cultivate resilience, patience, and a deeper appreciation for both the struggles and the joys that shape our journey.

Letting Go:

Mindful Practices for Your First Day

Before we dive into the exercises, let's take a moment to reflect on the power of journaling. Writing, whether it's a formal journal entry, a quick voice note on your mobile phone, or even a simple text to yourself, can be incredibly therapeutic. It's a way to give your thoughts a place to go, to clear mental space, and to express what you may not even realize you're carrying.

The beauty of journaling is that it doesn't have to be polished or perfect. It's about honesty, release, and acknowledging what's on your mind. So as we move into these writing exercises, know that there's no right or wrong way to express yourself—this is your moment of release.

Waves of Release:

What Are You Ready to Set Free?

Start by taking a deep breath and allowing yourself to fully arrive in the present moment. Now, think about everything you've been carrying with you—both physically and mentally. Write down all of the stressors, worries, obligations, and tasks that are lingering in your mind. Whether it's a work deadline, family responsibility, or something personal that's been weighing on you, put it all on paper.

Let it flow without judgment or editing. This exercise isn't about solving the problems or fixing the tasks, it's about acknowledging their presence and allowing yourself to release them, even just temporarily.

As you write, take your time. Don't rush to get everything down in one go. Think of this exercise as a form of self-compassion—allowing yourself to feel the relief of releasing the things that have been mentally draining you. You may be surprised by what comes up—things you didn't even realize were occupying your thoughts.

This is an opportunity to give your mind some space, to free up energy that you've been unconsciously holding onto. Writing it all down gives you permission to let go, even if just for today, and signals to your mind that it's okay to pause.

When you're finished writing, take a moment to breathe and recognize the power of this act. You have taken the first step toward releasing the mental clutter that may have followed you into this space. Reflect on how you feel after putting everything on paper. Does it feel like a weight has been lifted, even if only slightly?

This is just the beginning of your process, but already, you've made a meaningful shift by simply naming what you need to let go of. It's a powerful reminder that you don't have to carry everything with you—today, you are choosing to leave it behind.

This writing exercise allows you to be fully present with yourself and the moment. It's an opportunity to honor your feelings without judgment. If you find yourself coming up with a never-ending list of worries, know that this is normal.

The goal is not to eliminate them all at once but to acknowledge that they exist and that it's okay to step away from them for a little while. Once you've written everything down, take a moment to feel the space that's been created by releasing these thoughts. Your mental space is now open for relaxation and clarity.

Remember, the act of writing down your stressors is a gift to yourself. It's a way to clear your mental slate and give yourself permission to move into a more peaceful mindset. As you continue to unwind, keep in mind that this exercise is not just a one-time release—it can become a regular practice throughout your stay.

Each time you feel overwhelmed, return to this exercise and remind yourself that it's okay to let go.

Pinpointing Stressors:

A Reflective Exercise on Uncertainty

Now that you've acknowledged what you want to let go of, the next step is to dig deeper into what's truly stressing you out. Think about what feels uncertain or overwhelming in your life right now. Maybe it's work-related stress, a relationship challenge, or even the uncertainty of the future.

Write down the areas of your life that feel particularly challenging, the situations that leave you feeling uncertain or out of control. Don't censor yourself—this exercise is about bringing to light what's bothering you so that you can begin to address it with more awareness.

As you write, try to pinpoint the specific aspects of your stress. Is it the unknown that causes the most discomfort? The anticipation of something coming up in the future? Or is it the constant juggling of responsibilities that's creating mental clutter?

The goal of this exercise is not to solve the problems immediately, but rather to shine a light on the things that are causing you to feel uncertain. Sometimes just acknowledging these sources of stress can be a game-changer. Once they're written down, you can begin to distance yourself from them and realize that not everything needs to be solved right now.

This exercise is also a reminder that it's okay to have periods of uncertainty in life. No one has all the answers, and often, it's the unknown that creates the most stress. By writing down what feels uncertain, you're giving yourself permission to sit with it without needing to control it.

You're also inviting the opportunity for change by becoming aware of what's truly impacting your peace of mind. Recognizing the sources of your stress can be a powerful first step toward letting go of them and shifting into a more relaxed state of mind.

After you've identified the stressors, take a few moments to reflect on their importance. Are they things that need immediate attention, or can they be set aside for now? Sometimes, writing them down allows you to see them from a new perspective, and you may realize that some of these issues are out of your hands or can wait.

This is an empowering realization, as it allows you to reclaim your mental space and energy. Not everything needs to be tackled right away—sometimes, the most productive thing you can do is let go of the need to control everything.

Once you've written down your uncertainties, try to approach them with a sense of curiosity, rather than judgment. Reflect on how you can shift your relationship with these sources of stress.

Instead of seeing them as problems that must be solved immediately, you can choose to view them as challenges that will unfold in their own time.

This shift in mindset helps to ease the pressure you've been placing on yourself. Now, you can move into your reset with a lighter heart, knowing that you don't need to carry the burden of uncertainty.

Navigating the Unknown:

Reflecting on Life's Uncertainty

Now, let's reflect on the idea that uncertainty is a natural part of life. It's something we all experience, whether it's in our personal lives, our work, or in moments of transition like this one. The challenge is not to eliminate uncertainty but to accept it as part of the ebb and flow of life.

Think of the ocean. Sometimes the waves are calm, and other times, they're rough and unpredictable. But no matter the state of the water, the ocean always moves forward, adapting to whatever comes its way. Life is similar in that we can't always control what happens, but we can control how we respond to it.

Reflecting on this metaphor can help you shift your mindset around uncertainty. Instead of resisting it, accept that some things will remain unknown or out of your control. This doesn't mean giving up or ignoring the challenges in your life, but it does mean giving yourself permission to relax into the rhythm of life, just as the ocean does.

Like the waves, we may have moments of calm and moments of storm, but each phase will pass. By embracing uncertainty as a part of the journey, you can create more peace within yourself.

As you write, reflect on what it means to let go of the need for control. Sometimes, our stress comes from trying to manage the unmanageable. We worry about what's next, or about the things we cannot predict. But by allowing uncertainty to be a part of the experience, you give yourself the freedom to flow with it.

Much like the waves that come and go, the challenges in life will too. When you let go of the need to control everything, you make room for acceptance, peace, and a deeper sense of relaxation.

It's also important to recognize that accepting uncertainty doesn't mean you're resigned to helplessness. Instead, it's about embracing the natural flow of life and knowing that, even in times of challenge, there are opportunities for growth and learning.

Just as the ocean reshapes the shore over time, life's uncertainties can shape and refine you. By accepting this, you free yourself from the pressure of needing to have all the answers right now.

Finally, as you sit with this reflection, take a deep breath and remind yourself that it's okay not to know everything. You don't need to have all the answers to enjoy this moment, to be at peace, or to reset. The uncertainty is part of the beauty of life—the endless possibilities that unfold when we let go and allow the journey to unfold as it will.

Closing the Day with Gratitude

As Day 1 draws to a close, take a moment to acknowledge the small but powerful shift you've already made by stepping away from the rush of daily life. The act of arriving and settling in—whether through the mindful unpacking of your belongings, the creation of a serene space, or that refreshing first walk on the beach—sets the tone for the week ahead. These small rituals are more than just tasks; they are acts of intention, signals to your mind and body that it's time to let go of the stress you carried here.

Perhaps you took the time to reflect on what feels uncertain or heavy in your life right now. Writing these thoughts down may have felt like releasing a weight, even just a little. Embracing the natural rhythm of the ocean—its ebb and flow—can serve as a gentle reminder that uncertainty is an unavoidable, yet manageable, part of life. With each wave, imagine letting go of something you no longer need to carry.

As you settle into the slower pace of this new environment, allow yourself to feel the quiet satisfaction of a good beginning. You've already taken the first step toward a more peaceful state of mind. Let that accomplishment sink in as the sun sets, the day ends, and the promise of tomorrow stretches before you.

Day 2 ~

Shifting Sands:

Releasing What You Can't Control

Still Waters:

The Power of Mindfulness and Presence

Mindfulness and presence are essential practices in cultivating a peaceful and intentional life. In a world filled with distractions, the ability to focus on the present moment allows us to break free from the constant cycle of overthinking and worrying about the future. Day 2 invites us to explore the incredible power of mindfulness and the sovereignty of personal presence.

When we embrace mindfulness, we anchor ourselves in what is happening now, offering clarity and calm in the face of uncertainty. This connection to the present not only enhances our emotional well-being but also helps us appreciate the simple joys that often go unnoticed.

At its core, mindfulness is about tuning into our experiences without judgment. By paying attention to the details of our surroundings and our internal responses, we become more attuned to life as it unfolds. This practice fosters self-awareness, helping us identify what truly matters and let go of what doesn't serve us.

Mindfulness is not about ignoring challenges or avoiding discomfort; rather, it is about facing them with a grounded perspective, which can lead to more thoughtful and effective responses.

Presence is deeply intertwined with mindfulness, as it invites us to fully engage with the here and now. When we are present, we can savor the beauty of life's fleeting moments—whether it's the sound of waves, the warmth of the sun, or a conversation with a loved one.

By living in the moment, we free ourselves from the weight of regret and the pressure of anticipating what's to come. This practice encourages gratitude, reminding us that even the smallest experiences can be meaningful when we give them our full attention.

The importance of mindfulness and presence extends beyond our mental state; it also benefits our physical health. Studies have shown that mindfulness can reduce stress, lower blood pressure, and improve sleep.

By slowing down and focusing on the now, we allow our bodies and minds to recharge, creating a sense of balance that supports overall well-being. This balance is especially crucial in today's fast-paced world, where burnout and overwhelm are common challenges.

Cultivating mindfulness and presence is about creating a life that feels rich and intentional. These practices help us navigate the complexities of life with grace and resilience, providing a foundation for lasting peace.

By making a conscious effort to be mindful, we deepen our connection to ourselves, others, and the world around us. In doing so, we open the door to a more fulfilling and harmonious way of living.

Drifting into Serenity:

How Letting Go Brings Peace

Embracing the present moment and letting go of what lies beyond our control can profoundly transform our mindset, fostering a sense of peace and balance. When we focus on the here and now, we allow ourselves to fully experience life as it unfolds.

This practice shifts our attention away from regrets about the past or anxieties about the future, grounding us in the richness of the present. By releasing the weight of things we cannot change, we free up mental and emotional energy to engage more deeply with what truly matters.

One of the most significant benefits of embracing the moment is the clarity it brings. When we direct our attention to what is within our grasp, we become more intentional in our actions and decisions. This focus allows us to prioritize effectively, reducing feelings of overwhelm.

Conversely, dwelling on things outside our control often leads to frustration and helplessness. By accepting that some circumstances are beyond our influence, we can channel our energy toward meaningful pursuits that align with our values.

Letting go of uncontrollable factors also cultivates resilience. Life is full of uncertainties and challenges, but our response to them is what ultimately shapes our experience. When we learn to release control over the uncontrollable, we build mental strength and adaptability.

This mindset shift helps us approach obstacles with a sense of curiosity and resourcefulness rather than fear or defeat. Embracing this perspective empowers us to navigate difficulties with grace, knowing that we are equipped to handle whatever comes our way.

Embracing the moment also enhances our relationships with others. When we let go of trying to control external outcomes or other people's actions, we create space for acceptance and compassion.

This shift encourages deeper connections, as we approach interactions without the burden of unrealistic expectations or unnecessary judgments. By being fully present in our relationships, we foster trust and understanding, creating a more harmonious dynamic with those around us.

Ultimately, the combination of embracing the present and releasing what we cannot control leads to a more peaceful and fulfilled way of living. It allows us to find joy in the simplicity of life, whether through the sound of a gentle breeze or the warmth of a heartfelt conversation.

This approach not only enriches our daily experiences but also equips us to face life's challenges with a calm and grounded mindset. In letting go, we discover the freedom to live authentically and appreciate the beauty of the journey.

Calm Seas Ahead:

Grounding Yourself for the Day

Day 2 focuses on the transformative practice of reflection, grounding, and cultivating inner calm, all of which play an essential role in achieving balance and clarity in our lives. In the hustle and bustle of our daily routines, it's easy to lose sight of the present and get swept away by stressors that demand our attention. This day is designed to provide tools and practices that help us pause, reflect, and reconnect with our inner selves, allowing us to navigate life's challenges with greater ease and intention.

Reflection is a cornerstone of personal growth and self-awareness, and today we engage in meaningful introspection. By taking time to reflect on what we can control and what we cannot, we gain a clearer perspective on our priorities and limitations.

This exercise is not about dwelling on what's beyond our reach but about acknowledging it with acceptance. Through journaling and mindful contemplation, we can uncover valuable insights about our thoughts, emotions, and stressors, paving the way for more purposeful actions.

Grounding practices are another integral aspect of this day, offering a way to anchor ourselves in the present moment. Techniques such as mindfulness exercises, focusing on the breath, and connecting with nature—like feeling the sand beneath our feet or listening to the rhythm of ocean waves—help bring us back to a state of equilibrium.

Grounding serves as a reminder that no matter how chaotic life feels, we can always find stability within ourselves by returning to the present moment.

Cultivating inner calm is the ultimate goal here, and it ties together the practices of reflection and grounding. Inner calm doesn't mean eliminating stress entirely; rather, it's about learning to navigate life's ups and downs with grace and resilience.

By combining mindfulness and acceptance, we create a sense of peace that acts as a steady foundation, even in the face of uncertainty. This calmness allows us to approach challenges with a clear mind and an open heart, fostering a deeper connection to ourselves and our surroundings.

As we embark on our day, I invite you to embrace these practices as tools for inner transformation. Reflecting on what matters, grounding yourself in the present, and cultivating a sense of calm are powerful steps toward a more mindful and balanced life.

Today's journey is not just about letting go of external pressures but also about reclaiming your sense of peace and clarity. Through these practices, you'll discover a renewed sense of strength and serenity, preparing you to move forward with confidence and purpose.

The Wisdom of Sand Buckets: Simplifying Life's Challenges

Life can sometimes feel overwhelming, like a beach scattered with countless grains of sand representing our stressors. Sorting through them can seem impossible, but with the right approach, it becomes manageable.

Imagine a child on the beach with two sand buckets. One bucket is filled with sand they can lift and carry, and the other is so heavy with sand that they cannot. Similarly, we can sort our stressors into two categories: things we can control and things we can't. This simple yet powerful practice helps lighten the mental load and offers clarity in navigating challenges.

The first bucket represents the stressors we can control, much like the child carefully choosing how much sand to gather in their bucket for their sandcastle. These are the aspects of our lives where our actions and decisions make a difference—our responses, habits, and efforts.

Just as the child fills the bucket with just enough sand to lift, we can focus on what we can handle. This process empowers us, reminding us that we are not entirely at the mercy of life's chaos. By prioritizing these manageable stressors, we gain a sense of control and purpose.

The second bucket is for the stressors we cannot control, such as the tide washing away our sandcastle or the waves reshaping the shore. These represent external forces beyond our influence, like other people's actions, the passage of time, or unexpected events.

Acknowledging that these stressors belong in the "can't control" bucket frees us from the futile effort of trying to change them. Just as the child learns to leave behind the sand that is too heavy or unreachable, we too can release the burden of the uncontrollable.

This sorting process is not about denying the weight of what's in each bucket but about distributing it in a way that aligns with our abilities. The child doesn't try to carry several buckets at once, nor do they attempt to move the ocean! Instead, they focus on what they can manage and leave the rest to nature.

In the same way, we can give ourselves permission to let go of the things outside our control, redirecting our energy to what truly matters. By approaching stress with this mindset, we cultivate clarity and resilience. Sorting stressors into "can control" and "can't control" categories encourages us to act where we can and accept what we can't.

Like the child on the beach, we find peace not in controlling everything but in knowing where to focus our efforts. This practice helps lighten the emotional load, allowing us to move forward with strength and serenity.

Sailing Free:

Letting Go of What You Can't Control

Freedom often feels elusive in the face of life's uncertainties, but it can be found by letting go of what we cannot control. When we release the need to micromanage every aspect of our lives, we create space for peace and clarity.

This act of surrender does not mean giving up or ignoring challenges; rather, it's a shift in mindset that liberates us from unnecessary stress. By focusing only on what is within our power, we free ourselves to live more fully and authentically.

Letting go of the uncontrollable is akin to releasing a balloon into the sky. Holding onto it tightly only creates tension, while letting it drift away allows us to admire its journey without the burden of control.

In life, certain stressors, such as other people's actions or the unpredictability of nature, are beyond our influence. Obsessing over them drains our energy and prevents us from addressing what truly matters. Releasing these stressors lifts an invisible weight, offering a sense of emotional and mental lightness.

Freedom also comes from recognizing that the world is not ours to command. Trying to control external factors often leads to frustration and disappointment. Accepting life's uncertainties allows us to flow with its natural rhythms rather than resist them.

This perspective fosters a sense of harmony and connection, as we begin to trust in the unfolding of events rather than fight against them. With this trust, we gain the freedom to focus on our own growth and well-being.

The act of letting go is also deeply empowering. It shifts our focus from what we cannot change to what we can—our thoughts, actions, and reactions. This realization helps us reclaim our personal power, giving us the freedom to shape our responses and choices.

Instead of feeling trapped by circumstances, we become active participants in our lives, capable of adapting and thriving despite challenges. Ultimately, the freedom that comes from releasing control over the uncontrollable is a gift we give ourselves. It allows us to move through life with greater ease and less resistance.

By surrendering what we cannot change, we open the door to peace, clarity, and resilience. This act of release is not an admission of defeat but a bold step toward a life defined by balance and freedom. Incorporating a simple daily practice of sorting stressors into two categories—things you can control and things you cannot—is a transformative act that can reshape how we navigate life's challenges.

While it may seem like a small habit, its impact on mental clarity and emotional resilience is profound. By taking a few moments each day to reflect on what is within our power and what lies beyond it, we develop a mindset of acceptance and focus that fosters inner peace. This practice is remarkably accessible, requiring no special tools or extensive time commitments. All it takes is a few quiet minutes to sit with your thoughts and sort them into two mental "buckets."

By writing these stressors down or even visualizing them, you create a tangible sense of order amidst life's chaos. This process not only helps clear your mind but also reduces the overwhelming feeling that can come from facing too many uncertainties at once.

What makes this method transformative is its ability to shift our perspective over time. As we repeatedly identify and release what we cannot control, we begin to see patterns in our stress. Certain worries may resurface, but with regular practice, we learn to let go of them more quickly. Over time, this shift becomes second nature, allowing us to respond to challenges with greater calm and intentionality. Practice cultivates not only clarity but also resilience.

Another powerful aspect of this method is its adaptability. Whether you're at home, at work, or on the go, this exercise can be tailored to fit your day. It might take the form of journaling before bed, a mental check-in during a walk, or a moment of reflection while sipping your morning coffee. The simplicity of this practice ensures that it can easily become a seamless part of your routine, consistently guiding you toward balance and perspective.

Ultimately, adopting this practice is an investment in your emotional well-being. By taking a few moments each day to engage with your thoughts intentionally, you gain a sense of control over your mental space, even in the face of life's uncertainties.

This method is not about avoiding challenges but about empowering yourself to face them with a clear and composed mindset. Over time, the cumulative effects of this habit can lead to profound changes in how you approach life, transforming not only your relationship with stress but also your overall sense of peace and purpose.

Sunrise Serenity:

A Morning Mindfulness Practice

Starting the day with a mindful sunrise practice is a powerful way to set a peaceful and intentional tone for the hours ahead. The stillness of early morning, coupled with the gradual light of dawn, provides a natural backdrop for mindfulness. By taking the time to be present in this moment, you create space to connect with yourself and the world around you, fostering a sense of calm that can carry you through the day.

A mindful sunrise moment begins with finding a comfortable spot where you can observe the horizon. This could be on the beach, on the deck or in your backyard, or even by a window that offers a clear view.

As you settle in, take a few deep breaths, feeling the air fill your lungs and then gently leave your body. Allow yourself to focus entirely on the present, letting go of any lingering thoughts about the past or worries about the future.

This simple act of grounding prepares your mind to fully experience the beauty of the sunrise. As the first rays of sunlight begin to peek over the horizon, direct your attention to the colors and patterns unfolding before you. Notice the soft transitions of the sky—from deep blue to pink, orange, and gold. Listen to the sounds around you, whether it's the salty sea breeze, the calling of gulls, or the rhythmic crashing of waves. Feel the air on your skin and observe how the world slowly awakens. By engaging all your senses, you immerse yourself fully in the experience, deepening your connection to the moment.

This practice is more than just a morning ritual; it's a way to align your mind and body with the natural rhythm of the day. Observing the sunrise reminds you of life's cycles, the inevitability of change, and the promise of new beginnings. It encourages gratitude for the simple yet profound beauty of nature and offers a reminder to embrace life with openness and presence.

Carrying the mindfulness of a sunrise moment into your day can have lasting effects. The sense of peace and clarity gained in those quiet moments can act as a buffer against stress and distractions. It serves as a touchstone you can return to, simply by recalling the sunrise you witnessed. Starting the day with mindfulness isn't just an exercise; it's a declaration of your intention to approach life with grace and awareness, one moment at a time.

Calm Currents:

Using Mindfulness to Shape Your Day

Mindfulness plays a crucial role in setting a positive and intentional tone for the day, acting as a foundation for balance and clarity. By focusing on the present moment, mindfulness allows us to begin the day without the weight of past regrets or future anxieties. Instead, we can embrace the now, cultivating a sense of purpose and calm that influences how we navigate the hours ahead. This simple yet transformative practice creates space for intentional choices rather than reactive responses, empowering us to approach the day with a centered mindset.

One of the primary benefits of mindfulness in the morning is its ability to bring clarity and focus. In our fast-paced lives, it's easy to jump into the day overwhelmed by tasks and responsibilities. However, pausing to practice mindfulness helps quiet the noise, allowing us to prioritize what truly matters.

This sense of focus not only improves productivity but also reduces the mental clutter that often leads to stress. By starting with mindfulness, we create a mental roadmap for the day, ensuring our energy aligns with our goals and values.

Mindfulness also fosters gratitude, which is a key component of a positive outlook. When we pause to appreciate simple moments, like the warmth of sunlight or the stillness of morning, we set a tone of thankfulness that permeates the rest of the day.

Gratitude shifts our perspective, helping us to see challenges as opportunities and interactions as meaningful rather than mundane. This perspective is especially valuable when faced with unforeseen difficulties, as it enables us to respond with grace and resilience.

In addition, practicing mindfulness in the morning nurtures emotional balance. By taking time to breathe deeply, observe our thoughts, and connect with our emotions, we can better understand and manage how we feel. This self-awareness minimizes the likelihood of being swept away by stress or negativity later in the day. Instead, we carry a sense of calm that acts as a buffer against external pressures, helping us respond to situations with patience and composure.

Starting the day with mindfulness is more than a momentary exercise—it's a commitment to living with intention. It allows us to shape our day rather than be shaped by it, promoting a sense of agency and peace. By anchoring ourselves in the present and cultivating gratitude, focus, and emotional balance, mindfulness sets the stage for a day that is not only productive but also fulfilling and meaningful. This practice empowers us to move through life with clarity and purpose, one mindful moment at a time.

Golden Horizon:

Fully Embrace the Sunrise with These Tips

Engaging fully with the experience of the sunrise can set a calming and intentional tone for the day. To deepen your connection with this peaceful moment, follow these step-by-step guidelines for mindful observation:

1. Find a Comfortable Spot

Start by selecting a quiet, comfortable place to watch the sunrise, ideally somewhere with a clear view of the horizon. Sit or stand in a relaxed position, with your body open and relaxed. Allow your feet to connect to the earth, grounding yourself in the present moment. This will help create a peaceful setting for mindfulness.

2. Observe the Colors of the Sky

As the sun begins to rise, focus your attention on the changing colors in the sky. Notice how the light shifts from the soft, dim hues of dawn to the brilliant colors of the sun's first rays. Observe the transitions—pinks, oranges, yellows, and even purples—that fill the sky. Take your time to appreciate the subtle shifts in color, recognizing that each sunrise is unique.

3. Listen to the Sounds Around You

Shift your awareness to the sounds in your environment. The gentle crashing of waves, the rustle of the wind through the trees, or even the quiet hum of the earth waking up. Notice how the world around you seems to come alive during this time. The sounds of nature can be grounding and soothing, helping you connect with the present moment.

4. Feel the Good Morning Air

Pay attention to the sensation of the cool morning air against your skin. Breathe deeply, letting the fresh air fill your lungs. Feel the subtle chill in the atmosphere and how it shifts as the sun rises higher. By focusing on your breath and bodily sensations, you can enhance your mindfulness practice and bring your full attention to the present.

5. Reflect and Set Your Intentions for the Day

As the sunrise unfolds, take a moment to reflect on the beauty of the moment and what it signifies for your day ahead. Set a positive intention or affirmation for the day, focusing on qualities like patience, calmness, or gratitude. Let the serenity of the sunrise fill you with a sense of clarity and purpose, allowing you to begin the day with intention.

By engaging fully with the sunrise, you are not only connecting with nature but also cultivating mindfulness that will help guide you through the day with a calm, centered mindset.

Beachside Balance:

Activities to Ground You in the Present

As we discussed earlier, journaling is a powerful tool for self-reflection and emotional clarity, especially when it comes to managing stress and releasing unnecessary burdens. One effective journaling exercise involves writing two lists: one for what you can control and another for what you cannot.

This simple but transformative exercise helps you focus on the present moment and encourages mindfulness by acknowledging the limits of your influence. It provides both clarity and peace as you separate the areas of your life that are within your reach from those that are beyond your control.

To begin the exercise, grab a notebook or journal and divide the page into two columns. Label one column "What I Can Control" and the other "What I Cannot Control." Start by brainstorming and writing down everything that comes to mind.

In the "What I Can Control" column, list items like your actions, choices, attitudes, and responses to challenges.

These are aspects of life where you hold the power to make decisions and take intentional steps toward positive change. Examples might include how you react
to stressful situations, how much effort you put into your work, or how you maintain your health.

In the "What I Cannot Control" column, list things that are outside your direct influence. These might include other people's actions, weather conditions, the past, or unexpected circumstances. You might also note things like societal issues, other people's opinions, or the timing of events.

Recognizing these external factors can be a huge relief, as it highlights the areas where worrying or overthinking is unproductive. These are aspects of life that, while they may affect you, cannot be changed by your efforts.

Once you have written both lists, take a moment to reflect on the relief that comes from releasing control over the uncontrollable. Acknowledge how much energy and mental space is often consumed by stressors in the "What I Cannot Control" column. By recognizing what lies outside your grasp, you give yourself permission to let go.

This act of releasing is not about ignoring problems or being passive; rather, it's about accepting the natural ebb and flow of life and freeing yourself from unnecessary worry. The more you practice this, the lighter and more grounded you will feel.

This journaling exercise can become a daily or weekly practice that helps you regain focus and maintain mental clarity. Over time, you'll notice a sense of peace as you shift your energy from things that weigh you down to things that empower you.

The relief that comes from letting go of what you cannot control opens up space for personal growth, mindfulness, and a deeper connection to the present moment. By continuously returning to this practice, you learn to live more intentionally, focusing on the areas where you can make a positive impact and surrendering the rest.

The exercise of journaling about what you can and cannot control serves as a powerful reminder of the freedom that comes with releasing the things that are beyond your reach. By actively separating what is within your control from what is not, you create a sense of mental clarity and peace.

This practice encourages a mindset shift, helping you focus your energy on the areas of your life where you can make meaningful change while letting go of unnecessary stress. Regularly engaging in this journaling exercise can cultivate a sense of calm and intentionality, empowering you to navigate life with a lighter heart and a clearer mind.

Gentle Waves:

Finding Joy in Simple Moments

Savoring simple moments is an essential mindfulness practice that encourages you to focus on the sensory experiences around you. This exercise helps you cultivate presence by engaging all five senses and appreciating the beauty in even the most ordinary details of your environment. By consciously noticing textures, sounds, sights, and sensations, you slow down and create space to experience life more fully.

The practice of savoring encourages you to move beyond automatic routines and distractions, allowing you to connect deeply with the present moment. This shift in awareness can bring peace, reduce stress, and enrich your daily experiences.

To begin, start with a few deep breaths, grounding yourself in the present moment. As you take in your surroundings, choose one sense to focus on. For example, if you're near the beach, close your eyes for a moment and listen to the sound of the waves. Pay attention to the rhythm, the way the waves roll in and retreat, and how they shift in volume. Focus on how the sound resonates in your body, the calm it brings, and the stillness that settles in your mind. If you feel overwhelmed or distracted, take another deep breath to refocus.

Next, bring your attention to what you can feel. If you're sitting on the sand, observe the texture beneath you—whether it's coarse, smooth, warm, or cool. Imagine how the sand shifts with each movement, subtly adjusting as you settle in. Run your fingers through it or let it slip through your toes to deepen your tactile awareness. Be mindful of how it feels on your skin, noticing the sensation without judgment. This simple exercise can help you reconnect with your body and its immediate surroundings, fostering a greater sense of mindfulness.

Then, engage your sense of sight. Look at the colors in the sky or the shapes in the clouds. Notice how the light changes as the sun rises higher, casting golden hues or cool blues on the landscape. Observe the subtle beauty in the details around you—whether it's the texture of a leaf, the movement of the trees in the breeze, or the gentle flow of the water.

Take a moment to appreciate the visual richness of the world around you, which is often overlooked in the rush of everyday life. Let your eyes take in the beauty without judgment or expectation.

Finally, consider the warmth of the sun on your skin, or the coolness of the morning air. Feel the temperature changes as you sit in stillness, noticing how the environment shifts from cool to warm or vice versa. Let the physical sensations anchor you to the present, drawing your attention away from any worries or distractions.

By engaging with your environment through all your senses, you foster a deeper connection to the world around you, cultivating gratitude and presence in even the smallest moments.

Savoring simple moments through sensory awareness is a powerful way to reconnect with the present moment. By focusing on the sights, sounds, textures, and sensations around you, you can cultivate mindfulness and enhance your overall well-being.

This practice helps you slow down, savor the beauty in everyday life, and find peace in the simplicity of the world around you. With regular practice, savoring simple moments can become a natural part of your daily routine, offering moments of clarity and calm in the midst of life's busy pace.

Seashore Stillness:

A Practice in Grounding

Grounding practices are a powerful way to connect with the present moment and create a sense of stability and calm. By focusing on your breath and the physical sensations around you, you can shift your attention away from distractions and stressors, fostering a greater sense of presence and well-being.

One simple grounding exercise involves sitting on the sand, closing your eyes, and tuning into the sensations of the environment. This practice helps you establish a sense of connection with the earth and the space around you, encouraging mindfulness and emotional balance.

To begin the grounding practice, find a quiet spot on the sand where you feel comfortable and undisturbed. Sit down with your legs crossed or outstretched, allowing your body to settle into the earth. Gently close your eyes to eliminate visual distractions and begin to focus on your breath.

Take a slow, deep inhale, noticing the rise of your chest or abdomen. Exhale just as slowly, allowing any tension or distractions to melt away. Let each breath be a reminder that you are in the present moment, free from the pull of past worries or future concerns.

As you continue to focus on your breath, bring your awareness to the physical sensations beneath you. Feel the texture of the sand pressing against your body. Notice how the grains shift slightly as you adjust your posture. Feel the stability of the ground supporting you, offering a solid foundation.

The sand beneath you is constantly moving and shifting, yet it provides a sense of comfort and steadiness. This contrast allows you to connect with the earth's natural rhythms, helping you feel grounded and present in the moment.

Next, tune into the sensations around you. Pay attention to the temperature of the air on your skin, whether it's warm or cool. Notice any sounds nearby—the crash of the waves, the rustling of the wind, or the chirping of birds. These external sensations help you stay rooted in your current surroundings and reinforce your connection to the earth.

Let these sounds and feelings wash over you, allowing them to deepen your sense of calm and presence. As you focus on these sensations, you may notice that your thoughts slow down and become more focused.

Finally, bring your attention back to your breath, inhaling deeply and exhaling slowly. With each breath, feel a sense of peace settling deeper within you, connecting you to both your body and the earth.

The more you practice this grounding technique, the more natural it becomes to tap into this sense of stability and presence whenever you need it. Over time, it will help you navigate life's challenges with greater ease and clarity, allowing you to remain calm and centered in the face of stress.

Grounding practices are a simple yet effective way to cultivate mindfulness and presence. By connecting to your breath and tuning into the physical sensations around you, you foster a sense of stability and calm. This practice helps anchor you in the present moment, promoting emotional well-being and a greater connection to your surroundings. Whether you're sitting on the sand or in another environment, grounding exercises can provide a powerful tool for managing stress and enhancing your sense of peace and clarity.

Waves of Awareness:

Carrying Mindfulness Through Your Day

Mindfulness is the practice of being fully present and engaged in the moment, which can have a significant positive impact on our mental and emotional well-being. It encourages us to slow down and become more aware of our thoughts, feelings, and physical sensations, allowing us to experience life more deeply.

Practicing mindfulness throughout the day doesn't require a long, structured session; rather, it involves incorporating simple techniques into daily activities. By doing so, we can cultivate a sense of peace and presence that helps us manage stress and increase our overall happiness.

One effective strategy for practicing mindfulness throughout the day is to start by slowing down your actions. Whether you're eating, walking, or doing household chores, take the time to notice each movement. For example, when eating, focus on the taste, texture, and aroma of your food.

By savoring each bite and fully engaging your senses, you create an opportunity to pause and appreciate the present moment. This practice encourages you to step away from the rush of life and cultivate a deeper connection to what you're doing.

Another useful technique is to incorporate mindful breathing into your daily routine. Breathing deeply and intentionally can help center your thoughts and calm your mind. Whether you're at your desk, waiting in line, or walking to the car, take a few moments to focus on your breath.

Inhale slowly through your nose, hold for a moment, and exhale gently. This simple practice can reduce stress and help bring you back to the present when your mind starts to wander. By making mindful breathing a habit, you can shift your focus away from worries or distractions and improve your emotional well-being.

You can also practice mindfulness through your environment. Throughout the day, take time to notice your surroundings. Instead of letting your environment pass you by unnoticed, tune into the sights, sounds, and smells around you. When you're outside, observe the changing patterns of nature, the sound of birds, or the feeling of sunlight on your skin.

Even in indoor spaces, pay attention to the colors, textures, and sounds that surround you. Engaging with your environment helps you remain anchored in the present moment and encourages you to embrace life as it unfolds.

Additionally, practicing gratitude is an essential component of mindfulness. Throughout the day, take brief moments to reflect on the things you're grateful for. Whether it's something as simple as a good cup of coffee, a kind gesture from a friend, or a beautiful moment in nature, gratitude helps shift your focus away from negative thoughts and towards appreciation.

Journaling or even mentally acknowledging moments of gratitude can help reinforce a positive mindset, further encouraging mindfulness throughout the day.

Practicing mindfulness throughout the day doesn't require significant time or effort but can have profound effects on your overall well-being. By slowing down, breathing mindfully, engaging with your environment, and practicing gratitude, you can enhance your connection to the present moment.

These simple strategies offer valuable tools for managing stress and cultivating a greater sense of peace, allowing you to embrace everyday moments with awareness and intention. The more you integrate mindfulness into your daily life, the more you will experience its transformative benefits.

Drifting Free:

Easing Self-Judgment with Compassion

Self-judgment is an automatic response many of us have when we make mistakes or when things don't go as planned. It's easy to become our own harshest critics, often carrying unnecessary weight from past actions or future worries. However, self-judgment can create barriers to growth, self-compassion, and overall well-being.

Releasing self-judgment and approaching each moment with curiosity and openness allows us to experience life more fully and with greater acceptance. By adopting this mindset, we can transform negative self-talk into a more compassionate and constructive approach to life.

One way to release self-judgment is to practice self-compassion. When you catch yourself being critical, pause and ask yourself, "Would I say this to a friend?" Most likely, you would offer kindness and understanding instead of harshness.

Treating yourself with the same compassion you would give others allows you to shift away from judgment and towards self-acceptance. This doesn't mean ignoring mistakes but rather acknowledging them with understanding, offering yourself grace, and learning from the experience without feeling defeated or inadequate.

Another powerful way to release self-judgment is by cultivating curiosity. Curiosity is a mindset that invites you to explore rather than criticize. When something doesn't go as planned, instead of immediately placing blame or judging yourself, approach the situation with curiosity.

Ask yourself questions like, "What can I learn from this?" or "What's the opportunity for growth here?" By shifting your focus from judgment to exploration, you open up a space for self-discovery and growth, which allows you to see challenges as stepping stones rather than setbacks.

In addition, embracing openness is essential in releasing self-judgment. Openness involves accepting things as they are, without the need to control or change them immediately. By being open, you allow yourself to be in the moment, free of the constraints of past expectations or future anxieties.

When you approach situations with an open mind and heart, you are better able to accept yourself and others, finding peace in the flow of life rather than fighting against it. This openness creates an environment where mistakes are not failures but opportunities to grow, and where you can approach each new experience with a sense of freedom and possibility.

A gentle reminder to release self-judgment is to embrace the process of becoming, rather than striving for perfection. Life is full of moments that shape who we are, and it's important to remember that growth is a journey, not a destination.

Mistakes, successes, and everything in between contribute to our learning and development. Allowing yourself to be imperfect and human is part of the process. With each moment, choose to approach yourself and the world around you with curiosity, openness, and a willingness to learn, knowing that judgment only stands in the way of your true potential.

Releasing self-judgment and approaching each moment with curiosity and openness can profoundly change the way we experience life. By practicing self-compassion, fostering curiosity, and embracing openness, we shift our mindset from one of harsh critique to one of growth and acceptance.

This shift allows us to be more present, more at peace, and more aligned with our true selves. By incorporating these practices into your daily life, you can begin to break free from the grip of judgment and cultivate a deeper sense of freedom, understanding, and compassion for yourself and others.

Dusk on the Horizon:

Ending Our Day with Calm

As we wrap up our second day, let's take a moment to celebrate the progress we've made so far. Together, we've begun to feel the impact of our journey, building a foundation of mindfulness and intentional living.

We've explored the balance between acceptance and action—acknowledging what we cannot control while focusing our energy on what we can. Tools like the "two buckets" method have helped us sort through life's challenges, bringing clarity and calm to our minds and hearts.

Mindfulness invites us to slow down, be present, and engage with life more fully. It's a practice that transforms even the smallest moments into opportunities for peace and purpose. By integrating these lessons into our daily routines, we are already beginning to experience a shift—a sense of ease, resilience, and focus.

As the day ends on this gentle note, let's carry forward the lessons from Days 1 and 2, knowing that each step brings us closer to a life that feels authentic, manageable, and fulfilling. Together, we're creating something beautiful—a deeper connection to ourselves and the world around us.

Day 3 ~

Incoming Swells:

High Tides of Renewal

Surfing the Waves of Wellness

Rejuvenating both the body and mind is essential to maintaining a sense of balance and clarity. Physical health is intricately connected to mental well-being, and when we neglect one, it can affect the other. A healthy body fosters a clear mind, and a clear mind can guide a healthy body. This interconnectedness highlights the importance of physical renewal in any reset process.

By engaging in mindful movement and focusing on rejuvenating our bodies, we allow ourselves the space to let go of stress, build energy, and approach life with a fresh perspective. So on our Day 3, we explore how physical activity can release tension, increase vitality, and pave the way for greater mental clarity, all of which are essential elements in our journey of renewal.

Physical movement offers a powerful tool for reframing stress and building resilience. When life feels overwhelming, movement allows us to shift our perspective. Rather than seeing stress as something to avoid or eliminate, we can choose to view it as an opportunity for growth.

Activities like yoga, stretching, swimming, or walking provide moments of challenge, but these challenges are not obstacles; they are stepping stones toward greater strength. Every time we push ourselves to move our bodies, we challenge our perceptions of our own limitations. With each movement, we break down the barriers that stress erects in our minds, and we build resilience.

As we embrace these challenges, we also open ourselves to growth, understanding that, like the ebb and flow of the ocean's waves, every challenge we face contributes to our strength.

The ocean, with its rhythmic waves, provides a perfect environment for physical and mental renewal. Swimming in the ocean is not just a form of exercise—it is an experience that engages both the body and the mind. The natural resistance of the water makes every stroke feel like a workout, but with each movement, we strengthen our muscles and calm our minds.

Swimming can feel like an act of meditation; as the waves move in and out, so do our thoughts and worries. Just like the ocean, we learn that our strength builds over time, through repetition and consistent effort.

Yoga and walking on the beach offer similar benefits. Both activities connect us to the natural world and help us become more mindful of our bodies, whether we're stretching under the morning sun or walking along the shore, taking in the sights and sounds around us.

Simple stretches and yoga poses on the beach provide a wonderful way to start the day and connect with our bodies. These practices are an accessible means of releasing the tension that accumulates in our muscles and mind. The beach setting is perfect for these exercises, as the sand grounds us and the sounds of the ocean create a peaceful backdrop.

By focusing on areas of the body that tend to hold tension—such as the back, shoulders, hips, and legs—we give ourselves the opportunity to release not only physical discomfort but also mental and emotional stress. With each stretch, we are reminded to listen to our bodies and treat them with the care they deserve. The gentle movements offer a chance to reflect on our own well-being and set the tone for the rest of the day.

Today, we encourage embracing the rhythm of life, where both movement and stillness have their place. By integrating simple yoga, swimming, or walking into your day, you begin to build a foundation for resilience, strength, and mindfulness.

As you move through these practices, remember that challenges are not to be feared but embraced. They are the catalysts for growth and the foundation of resilience. By finding excitement in these challenges and allowing your body to move freely, you cultivate a deeper understanding of your own strength and capacity. The more you engage with your body in this way, the more you'll realize that, just like the ocean, you have the ability to rise and fall with the waves, learning and growing with every movement.

Calming the Storm Within

Stress is a common part of daily life, and its effects can manifest in both the body and the mind. When we're stressed, our bodies often respond with physical tension, such as tight muscles, shallow breathing, and a racing heart. However, physical movement provides a powerful tool for reframing stress. By engaging in physical activity, we can shift our mental state, reduce tension, and restore a sense of balance. Movement acts as a bridge between our physical and mental well-being, helping to transform the negative effects of stress into positive, restorative energy.

One of the key ways physical movement can help reframe stress is through its ability to activate the body's relaxation response. Activities like stretching, yoga, or walking can calm the nervous system and reduce the physical symptoms of stress. When we focus on our breath while moving, we activate the parasympathetic nervous system, which counters the fight-or-flight response.

This process not only relaxes the body but also creates mental clarity, helping us gain perspective on stressful situations. The simple act of moving—whether it's a gentle stretch or a brisk walk—can shift our mind away from stress and into a more grounded, present state.

Movement also provides an outlet for the energy that stress generates. Stress often leads to a build-up of tension in the body, and without an outlet, that tension can become overwhelming. Engaging in physical activities like running, swimming, or dancing helps to release this built-up energy, which can help relieve feelings of stress and frustration.

As we move our bodies, we begin to feel lighter, both physically and mentally, which can help break the cycle of negative thinking that often accompanies stress. By focusing on the movement itself, we allow our minds to shift away from the stressor and redirect our energy toward something positive.

Physical movement encourages mindfulness, which can be especially helpful in reframing stress. Mindfulness involves being fully present in the moment, observing what is happening in and around us without judgment. When we move, we can focus our attention on the sensations in our body—the stretch of our muscles, the rhythm of our breath, and the sound of our movements.

This focus helps us detach from stressful thoughts and emotions, allowing us to experience the present moment without the weight of anxiety or worry. Through mindful movement, we can create space between ourselves and our stress, promoting mental clarity and calmness.

Regular physical movement strengthens our resilience to stress over time. When we make movement a habit, we develop the ability to cope with stress more effectively. The more we engage in physical activity, the better we become at handling stress in a healthy way.

By shifting our perspective from stress as something to avoid or fear to something we can manage through movement, we empower ourselves to face challenges with strength and resilience. In this way, physical movement becomes not just a tool for reducing stress, but a way to build long-term emotional and physical well-being.

Anchored in Strength

Resilience, the ability to recover from setbacks and adapt to challenges, is a vital quality for both the body and mind. With schedules that feel endless and time that feels fleeting, stressors can come from various sources—work, relationships, or personal struggles—and it's essential to develop tools to manage these difficulties.

One of the most effective ways to build resilience is through physical activity. Engaging in regular movement helps not only to strengthen the body but also to bolster mental fortitude. As we move, our bodies and minds work together, cultivating resilience that helps us face life's obstacles with greater ease.

Physical activity offers numerous benefits that contribute to resilience. It strengthens muscles, improves cardiovascular health, and enhances flexibility, all of which prepare the body to endure stress. Beyond the physical benefits, exercise helps regulate stress hormones, reduces anxiety, and improves sleep—factors that contribute to better mental health.

By integrating movement into daily life, we develop both physical and emotional resilience. Our bodies become more capable of handling stress, and our minds become more adept at navigating challenges with a calm, focused approach.

Engaging in physical activity also fosters a mindset of perseverance. As we push through physical challenges—whether it's a long walk, a tough workout, or a challenging yoga session—we teach ourselves the value of persistence. Each movement and effort helps us build confidence in our ability to overcome difficulty.

When we encounter obstacles, whether in exercise or life, we begin to recognize that we have the strength to keep going. This connection between physical exertion and mental strength reinforces our resilience, enabling us to handle adversity with a positive, determined outlook.

Physical movement can also provide a sense of control and empowerment. When life feels overwhelming, taking charge of our bodies through exercise allows us to regain a sense of agency. The act of moving—whether through running, swimming, or dancing—gives us a tangible way to release built-up tension and stress.

It empowers us to act, rather than feel passive in the face of adversity. Regular exercise reminds us that we can control our actions and our responses, even when other aspects of life may feel uncertain or outside of our control.

Building resilience through physical activity is about consistency. Just as resilience in life requires time and practice, so does resilience in the body and mind. The more regularly we engage in physical activity, the stronger and more adaptable we become. Over time, physical activity helps build a foundation of mental toughness, allowing us to bounce back more quickly from challenges and maintain a sense of balance even in difficult times.

Riding the Waves of Mental Fortitude

Regular physical movement is often seen as a way to improve physical health, but its long-term benefits extend far beyond the body. Exercise plays a crucial role in building emotional and mental resilience, equipping individuals to better handle stress, overcome challenges, and maintain a positive outlook on life.

By engaging in consistent movement, whether through walking, running, swimming, or yoga, we create a foundation for both physical strength and emotional stability. The long-term effects of regular movement help cultivate a mindset that can persevere through difficulties and bounce back from setbacks with greater ease.

One of the most significant benefits of regular physical activity is its positive impact on mental health. Exercise is known to trigger the release of endorphins, which are chemicals in the brain that act as natural mood boosters. These endorphins help reduce stress, anxiety, and depression, all of which can undermine emotional resilience.

By engaging in movement consistently, the brain becomes more adept at managing stress, resulting in a greater capacity to cope with life's challenges. Over time, regular exercise can help individuals develop a more balanced emotional state, allowing them to approach difficult situations with a clearer and calmer mindset.

Physical movement also enhances emotional resilience by promoting better sleep, reducing tension, and improving overall energy levels. Sleep is crucial for emotional regulation, and regular exercise has been shown to improve sleep quality. With better rest, the body and mind are better prepared to handle stress, reducing emotional reactivity and promoting stability.

Movement also helps to release pent-up stress and tension in the body, making it easier to stay grounded and centered during challenging moments. As individuals continue to practice regular movement, they build a stronger foundation of emotional resilience that allows them to remain calm and focused, even in high-pressure situations.

Beyond the physical and emotional benefits, regular movement also fosters mental resilience by promoting a growth mindset. Engaging in physical activity requires persistence and discipline, and over time, individuals learn to push through challenges and setbacks.

This mental toughness developed through consistent exercise translates into other areas of life, where individuals are more likely to persevere when faced with obstacles. As the body grows stronger and more capable through regular movement, the mind follows suit, adopting a mindset that views challenges as opportunities for growth and development.

Best of all, the long-term benefits of regular movement extend to building a sense of self-efficacy and confidence. When individuals commit to regular physical activity, they begin to see the tangible results of their efforts, whether in improved fitness levels, increased energy, or a greater sense of well-being.

These accomplishments reinforce a positive self-image, building the belief that one is capable of handling whatever challenges come their way. As this confidence grows, so too does emotional and mental resilience, creating a powerful cycle of growth and empowerment.

Beach-Friendly Stretches and Yoga Poses

Beach-friendly stretches and yoga poses are an excellent way to start the day with intention, mindfulness, and physical rejuvenation. The beach setting adds an extra layer of tranquility and connection to nature, making it the perfect environment to engage in stretches and yoga that ground your body and mind.

The natural elements—the sound of the waves, the cool sand beneath your feet, and the open sky above—create a peaceful atmosphere that enhances the experience of stretching and moving. By incorporating these gentle exercises into your morning routine, you create a moment of clarity and balance to begin the day with fresh energy.

To start, try a simple seated stretch. Sit comfortably on the sand, with your legs extended out in front of you. Inhale deeply, lengthening your spine, and then exhale, reaching forward toward your toes or the sand in front of you. Focus on the stretch along your back and legs, while keeping your breath steady and calm.

This stretch not only helps release tension from your body but also promotes mindfulness as you focus on each movement and breath. As you hold this pose for a few breaths, notice how your body responds, and gently deepen the stretch if it feels right.

Next, try the classic Downward-Facing Dog pose, which is a staple in many yoga routines and great for stretching multiple areas of the body. Start on all fours with your hands and knees on the sand, ensuring that your wrists are directly under your shoulders and your knees are under your hips.

On your inhale, lift your hips toward the sky, creating an inverted "V" shape with your body. Press your heels gently into the sand while reaching your hands forward. This pose stretches the back, shoulders, and hamstrings, while also strengthening your arms and core. Stay in the pose for several deep breaths, allowing your body to lengthen and release any tension.

Another great beach-friendly stretch is the seated side stretch. Sit cross-legged on the sand or with your legs extended, and gently reach one arm overhead, bending to the opposite side. Keep your other hand on the sand for balance and stability.

This stretch helps open up the sides of the body and increases flexibility in the torso, hips, and shoulders. While in the stretch, focus on lengthening your body with each inhale and deepening the stretch with each exhale. Repeat on the other side, and allow your body to feel more open and relaxed after each stretch.

Finally, a gentle Warrior pose (Virabhadrasana) is perfect for building strength and stability. Start by standing tall, feet spread wide apart, and turning one foot outward at a 90-degree angle. Extend your arms out to the sides, parallel to the sand, and bend your front knee to a 90-degree angle while keeping your back leg straight. Gaze over your front hand and hold the pose for several breaths.

This standing pose strengthens the legs, opens the hips, and builds endurance while grounding your body in the present moment. Repeat on the other side to ensure both sides are equally stretched and strengthened.

Beach-friendly stretches and yoga poses offer an ideal way to start the day with mindfulness and physical renewal. By incorporating simple stretches and yoga poses such as seated stretches, Downward-Facing Dog, seated side stretches, and Warrior poses, you not only awaken your body but also connect with the natural surroundings. These exercises help release tension, improve flexibility, and enhance overall well-being.

Whether you are a seasoned yogi or a beginner, practicing these movements on the beach or balcony or deck allows you to enjoy the benefits of mindful movement while soaking in the beauty of your surroundings. With each stretch and pose, you set a positive tone for the day, cultivating a sense of calm, strength, and intention.

Stretching with the Tide

Gentle stretches can be incredibly beneficial for relieving tension in areas of the body that often hold stress, such as the back, shoulders, hips, and legs. These areas are commonly affected by poor posture, long hours of sitting, or even emotional stress. Engaging in targeted stretches not only helps alleviate discomfort but also promotes flexibility, enhances blood flow, and improves overall mobility. By incorporating simple, mindful stretches into your routine, you can address areas of tension in a gentle, effective way, ultimately fostering both physical and mental relaxation.

One of the most common areas of tension is the back, especially the lower back, which can become stiff from prolonged sitting or poor posture. A simple stretch for this area is the Cat-Cow Stretch, which helps improve flexibility and alleviate tightness in the spine.

To perform this stretch, start on all fours, with your hands under your shoulders and knees under your hips. As you inhale, arch your back, lifting your chest and tailbone toward the sky (Cow position), and as you exhale, round your back, tucking your chin to your chest (Cat position). This fluid movement helps stretch and strengthen the muscles in the back, while also promoting spinal mobility and relaxation.

The shoulders are another area where tension often accumulates, especially for people who carry stress in their upper bodies. A great stretch for the shoulders is the Shoulder Rolls. To perform this stretch, simply sit or stand tall, inhale deeply, and as you exhale, roll your shoulders forward in a circular motion. After a few rolls, reverse the direction, rolling your shoulders backward.

This gentle motion helps to release tension in the shoulders, neck, and upper back, while also improving circulation and range of motion. It's an excellent stretch to incorporate throughout the day, especially if you find yourself sitting for long periods.

For the hips, which can tighten up from sitting for long hours or from certain types of physical activity, the Seated Figure Four Stretch is an effective way to release tightness and improve flexibility. To perform this stretch, sit in a chair or on the floor and cross one ankle over the opposite knee, creating a figure-four shape with your legs. Gently press the raised knee away from your body to deepen the stretch in the hip and outer thigh. This stretch helps open up the hip flexors, glutes, and lower back, areas that are commonly tight for many people. Hold the stretch for 30 seconds to 1 minute on each side to achieve maximum relief.

Leg tension can result from both sitting and standing for extended periods, and stretching the hamstrings and quadriceps can help release this built-up stress. One simple stretch to release tension in the legs is the Standing Hamstring Stretch. Begin by standing tall and extending one leg straight out in front of you with your heel on the ground and toes pointing upward. Gently hinge at your hips, lowering your torso toward the extended leg while keeping your back straight.

This stretch targets the hamstrings and can help improve flexibility in the legs, reducing stiffness. You can also stretch the quadriceps by gently pulling one foot toward your glutes while standing, holding your ankle with your hand. This stretches the front of the thigh, relieving tightness that can occur from activities such as running or walking.

Incorporating gentle stretches into your daily routine can provide numerous benefits for areas of tension in the body, such as the back, shoulders, hips, and legs. By focusing on specific stretches like the Cat-Cow Stretch, Shoulder Rolls, Seated Figure Four, and Standing Hamstring Stretch, you can release tightness, improve flexibility, and reduce discomfort.

These simple yet effective exercises promote both physical and mental relaxation, helping you feel more balanced and centered. Practicing these stretches regularly allows you to alleviate tension and support your body's overall health, helping you move with ease and confidence throughout your day.

Tides of Tranquility:

Finding Peace Through Movement

Being near the ocean offers a unique and calming environment that can enhance any yoga or mindfulness practice. The rhythmic sound of the waves, the fresh scent of the sea air, and the vastness of the horizon all work together to create a sense of peace and tranquility. These natural elements have long been associated with relaxation and stress reduction, making the beach an ideal setting for cultivating mindfulness and connection.

Practicing yoga by the water not only provides physical benefits but also nurtures a peaceful state of mind, making it a powerful way to connect with both your body and the environment around you.

One of the primary ways the ocean enhances a yoga practice is through its calming sounds. The gentle crashing of waves creates a natural soundtrack that can help quiet the mind, allowing you to focus more fully on your breath and movements. This sound has a meditative quality, drawing your attention away from distractions and encouraging a deep sense of presence in the moment.

Whether you're in a restorative pose like Child's Pose or a more active one like Downward Dog, the sound of the ocean helps ground you and fosters a sense of relaxation, reducing stress and promoting inner peace.

The cool, salty air near the ocean also contributes to the calming effects of a beachside yoga practice. Breathing in the fresh sea air helps clear the mind and refreshes the body, providing a sense of vitality. As you inhale deeply, the natural environment around you supports your breath, making it easier to relax into each pose.

The combination of fresh air and physical movement encourages deep breathing, which enhances relaxation and reduces tension. This creates an environment where both your body and mind can unwind and release any stress or tightness.

The ocean's vastness also provides a feeling of expansiveness, both physically and mentally. The endless horizon invites a sense of openness, creating space in the mind to let go of worries and be fully present. This connection to something larger than yourself can help you feel more grounded and centered in your practice.

It also provides an opportunity for reflection and release, as the ocean symbolizes the flow of life and the ebb and flow of emotions. Just as the tides rise and fall, you can learn to embrace the rhythm of your breath and movement, letting go of what no longer serves you.

Additionally, the natural beauty of the beach fosters a sense of connection to the earth. Whether you're practicing near the water's edge or on soft sand, being in direct contact with nature helps you feel rooted and present. The textures of the sand beneath your feet, the warmth of the sun on your skin, and the sight of the ocean create a sensory experience that encourages mindfulness.

This sensory awareness deepens your connection to the present moment and enhances the calming effect of the practice. The beach becomes a sanctuary where you can slow down, connect with your breath, and cultivate peace of mind.

Seashells and Stretches:

Capturing the Shift Within

Starting a mindful practice of yoga and stretching is a great way to connect with your body and promote physical and mental well-being. However, one of the most effective ways to deepen your practice and increase awareness of its benefits is to take time afterward to journal about your experience.

Reflecting on how your body feels before and after stretching helps you to track changes in your physical state and observe any emotional shifts that may occur. By incorporating this simple journaling exercise, you can gain valuable insight into how stretching impacts your body and mind, allowing you to enhance your self-care routine.

Before you begin your stretches, take a moment to check in with your body. Sit comfortably and take a few deep breaths to tune into how your body feels. Notice areas of tension or tightness, particularly in common problem areas like the shoulders, back, hips, or legs.

Record these observations in your journal, writing down any discomfort or stiffness you may be feeling. This pre-stretch assessment sets the stage for noticing improvements after your session and gives you a clearer understanding of how your body responds to the stretching exercises.

As you proceed with your stretches, focus on the sensations in your body. Whether you are practicing simple stretches or more advanced yoga poses, pay attention to how your muscles feel as they lengthen and relax. Notice the feeling of release or tension in specific areas and be mindful of your breath.

This presence during your stretches helps foster a deeper connection to your body. Keep in mind that this experience is not about pushing yourself too hard but rather listening to what your body needs in the moment. After your session, take a moment to reflect on how your body feels after completing your stretches.

Once you've finished your stretches, sit quietly again and notice any changes in your body. Do you feel more relaxed or more energized? Is there less tension in your shoulders, back, or legs? Perhaps you feel lighter or more flexible. Write these observations in your journal, reflecting on the differences between how you felt before and after stretching.

This exercise helps highlight the benefits of stretching and makes you more aware of how your body responds to movement. It also provides an opportunity to acknowledge any progress, no matter how small, and to celebrate the positive effects of taking time for yourself.

Journaling after your stretches also encourages a sense of gratitude for your body and the work it does. As you reflect on the improvements in your flexibility or the release of tension, you cultivate a greater appreciation for your body's capabilities.

Over time, journaling can become an essential part of your stretching routine, helping you develop a deeper understanding of how your body functions and how to care for it. This process not only fosters physical well-being but also promotes a positive mindset and a sense of self-care.

Saltwater Serenity:

The Dual Benefits of Ocean Swimming

Ocean swimming is an excellent activity that offers both physical exercise and mental clarity. The combination of the rhythmic motion of swimming and the calming sound of the waves provides a unique opportunity to connect with nature while benefiting both the body and the mind.

The ocean's cool, refreshing water makes swimming an invigorating workout, while its vast, peaceful surroundings foster a sense of tranquility and mindfulness. Whether you are a seasoned swimmer or a beginner, incorporating ocean swimming into your routine can be a fulfilling practice that nurtures both physical health and mental well-being.

Physically, swimming in the ocean is a full-body workout that engages multiple muscle groups. The resistance of the water builds strength and endurance, while the buoyancy helps reduce stress on the joints, making it an ideal exercise for people of all fitness levels.

Swimming provides a cardiovascular workout that improves heart health and increases lung capacity. The natural resistance of the ocean waves adds an element of challenge, helping you build muscle tone and increase flexibility. By regularly swimming in the ocean, you can improve overall fitness, boost energy levels, and maintain a healthy weight.

On the mental side, ocean swimming offers a unique opportunity to meditate and clear your mind. The sound of the waves crashing and the feeling of being immersed in the natural world help create a peaceful environment that encourages mindfulness. As you swim, you can focus on your breath and the rhythm of your strokes, which allows you to enter a meditative state.

The repetitive motion of swimming can have a calming effect, reducing stress and promoting a sense of mental clarity. The vastness of the ocean also helps you put things into perspective, allowing you to release worries and return to a sense of balance.

In addition to its mental and physical benefits, ocean swimming encourages a deep connection to nature. The feeling of being in the water, surrounded by the open sea, can be humbling and awe-inspiring. The vastness of the ocean fosters a sense of freedom, and the natural world offers a reminder of life's simplicity and beauty.

Swimming in the ocean provides an opportunity to disconnect from the distractions of daily life and reconnect with the earth's rhythms, helping to ground and center your thoughts. This connection to nature can inspire gratitude and mindfulness, creating a sense of peace and well-being that extends beyond the swim.

To incorporate ocean swimming into your routine, it is helpful to follow a few simple guidelines. Start by warming up your body with gentle stretches to prepare your muscles for the cool water. If you are new to ocean swimming, begin with short swims in shallow water and gradually build your confidence and endurance. Focus on your breath as you swim, taking slow, deep breaths in sync with your strokes. Allow your body to flow with the rhythm of the waves, maintaining a relaxed and steady pace. After your swim, take time to reflect on how the experience made you feel, both physically and mentally. This reflection will help you recognize the calming and energizing effects of ocean swimming.

Power, Stamina, and Flow:

Benefits of Swimming in the Sea

Swimming in the ocean provides a wealth of physical benefits that go beyond the standard advantages of swimming in a pool. The natural environment of the ocean offers resistance that can enhance the effectiveness of your workout, while also providing a unique, low-impact experience.

The coolness of the water, combined with the natural resistance of the waves, creates an ideal environment for improving cardiovascular fitness, building strength, and increasing endurance. These benefits make ocean swimming an excellent choice for anyone looking to improve their overall health, fitness, and well-being.

One of the primary benefits of ocean swimming is the building of strength. As you swim, your body works against the natural resistance of the water, which engages various muscle groups. The resistance provided by the water is constant and effective, making it possible to build strength in both the upper and lower body.

Whether you are performing freestyle, breaststroke, or treading water, each stroke activates muscles in your arms, legs, and core. Over time, regular ocean swimming will help tone muscles, increase muscle endurance, and enhance overall physical strength.

Endurance is another area that is significantly improved through ocean swimming. Unlike traditional swimming in a pool, where the water is still and predictable, the ocean introduces varying conditions, such as waves, currents, and tides. This unpredictability challenges your body in new ways, forcing it to adapt and become more resilient.

Swimming against waves, for example, requires more effort and engages your cardiovascular system at a higher level, which boosts stamina and endurance. As you continue to swim in the ocean, you'll notice your ability to swim longer distances or tackle more challenging conditions without tiring as quickly.

In addition to building strength and endurance, ocean swimming is an excellent way to enhance circulation. The cool temperature of the water causes your blood vessels to constrict, which increases blood flow to your vital organs. This natural process helps improve circulation throughout the body, ensuring that oxygen and nutrients are delivered efficiently to your muscles and tissues.

Enhanced circulation can also promote faster recovery after exercise, reduce muscle soreness, and improve overall heart health. Regular ocean swimming can be a powerful tool for boosting circulation, improving heart function, and promoting overall cardiovascular health.

The added benefit of swimming in the ocean is the mental relaxation and connection to nature it provides. Unlike a pool, the ocean environment encourages mindfulness as you focus on the rhythm of the waves, your breath, and the surrounding beauty. The natural environment fosters a sense of calm and peace, helping to reduce stress and improve overall mental well-being. By swimming in the ocean, you are not only strengthening your body and improving circulation but also fostering a deep connection to the natural world, which can contribute to emotional healing and tranquility.

Guided by the Tide:
Ocean Swimming Made Simple

Warm-Up: Start with light stretches or a gentle walk on the beach to prepare your muscles for the swim.

Start Slow: Begin by swimming in shallow water to get used to the temperature and conditions. Gradually increase the distance as you build confidence.

Focus on Technique: Maintain proper swimming form, ensuring you're using your arms, legs, and core effectively to maximize strength-building.

Pace Yourself: Swim at a steady pace that allows you to focus on your breathing and maintain endurance.

End with a Cool-Down: After your swim, take a few minutes to walk along the shore and allow your body to adjust to the temperature change.

Breath, Movement, and Mind: The Meditative Flow of Swimming

Swimming in the ocean offers a unique experience that blends physical exercise with mental relaxation, making it an ideal practice for those seeking to reduce stress and clear their mind. The rhythm of swimming, particularly when combined with controlled breathing, is similar to meditation in many ways.

Just as in meditation, swimming encourages focus and presence, allowing you to shut out external distractions and become fully immersed in the activity. This connection between breath and movement provides a meditative quality, allowing the swimmer to achieve mental clarity while simultaneously benefiting from the physical workout.

The first way swimming aligns with meditation is through the focus on breath. In both practices, breathing is central to maintaining calm and enhancing concentration. When swimming, the rhythm of breathing—whether you're doing front crawl, breaststroke, or another stroke—becomes a steady, calming rhythm that mirrors the breath-focused techniques used in meditation.

By syncing your breath with your movements, you naturally calm your mind and body. As with deep breathing exercises in meditation, controlled breaths help to regulate stress levels and reduce anxiety, promoting a state of relaxation and mental clarity.

The fluidity of movement in swimming also plays a crucial role in creating a meditative experience. Swimming allows for a continuous flow of motion, much like the flow of thoughts in meditation. As you swim, your body moves through the water with each stroke, creating a rhythmic cycle of action and rest. This movement provides a sense of grounding and presence, similar to the way a focused meditation practice helps to anchor thoughts and promote mindfulness.

The repetitive nature of swimming encourages a mental state where you can disconnect from external stressors and focus solely on the task at hand, whether it's completing a lap or simply feeling the rhythm of your body in the water.

Furthermore, swimming in the ocean adds an element of nature that enhances the meditative experience. The sound of the waves, the sensation of water against your skin, and the vastness of the ocean can all be considered natural forms of sensory input that deepen the mindfulness practice.

Just like in meditation, where practitioners use the sound of a bell or a mantra to deepen their focus, the natural sounds and sensations of swimming in the ocean provide a peaceful environment that aids in reducing mental clutter. The water's movement encourages a sense of flow, while the quiet environment allows for inner stillness, helping swimmers reconnect with themselves and experience a calming, meditative state.

By combining movement with breath and immersing yourself in the natural world, swimming becomes a holistic practice that nurtures both mind and body. As with meditation, swimming creates a space for mindfulness, helping to clear mental clutter and focus on the present moment.

It offers a low-impact exercise that strengthens muscles, improves cardiovascular health, and reduces stress while also promoting emotional and mental clarity. Regularly engaging in this rhythmic form of movement can reduce anxiety, improve mood, and enhance overall well-being.

Water's Whisper:
Simple Guidelines for Swimming with Intention

Focus on Breath: Begin by finding a steady rhythm of breathing, matching each breath with your strokes. Focus on deep, slow inhales and exhales to help calm the mind.

Establish a Smooth Rhythm: Pay attention to the fluidity of your strokes and allow your body to move through the water without strain. Let the natural flow of the water guide your movements.

Be Present: As you swim, keep your attention on the sensations in your body, the movement of the water, and the sounds around you. Try to let go of any distractions and focus only on the present moment.

Swim at Your Own Pace: There's no need to rush. Swim at a comfortable pace, allowing yourself to get lost in the rhythm of breath and movement.

End with a Cool-Down: After your swim, take a few moments to float or rest on the shore. Pay attention to how your body feels, taking note of any changes in how you feel mentally and physically.

The Rhythm of Resilience:
Lessons from the Waves

Swimming in the ocean offers a unique opportunity to combine physical exercise with mental clarity. The natural resistance of water provides a full-body workout that helps build strength and endurance, while the rhythmic nature of swimming encourages relaxation and stress relief.

As you swim, your muscles engage, and your heart rate increases, improving circulation and helping to reduce the tension that builds up in the body from daily stressors. The challenge of moving through the water, while constantly adapting to its fluctuations, mirrors how we can navigate life's challenges with greater ease and strength when we stay grounded and adaptable.

One of the most powerful aspects of swimming in the ocean is the constant movement of the water, which symbolizes the ebb and flow of life's challenges. Just as the waves rise and fall, life's difficulties come and go. By swimming through the waves, you practice how to face these challenges with resilience.

The key to swimming with ease is not to fight the waves, but to move with them. This is a valuable lesson for how we can approach life's obstacles—by learning to adapt and flow with the changes rather than resisting them, we gain strength and become more capable of navigating difficult situations.

As you swim, you will notice how the water's resistance requires you to exert more effort, but the results are rewarding. Similarly, facing life's challenges requires effort and energy, but the outcome can lead to personal growth and emotional strength. The resistance of the water pushes you to build strength, just as facing adversity in life can lead to resilience and greater self-awareness.

Swimming through the waves reminds us that every challenge, no matter how difficult, is an opportunity for growth and empowerment. With each stroke, you become more aware of your body's capacity to handle resistance, which can parallel your mental capacity to manage stress and uncertainty.

The act of swimming also encourages a deep sense of mindfulness, where you focus on your breath and body movements to stay in rhythm with the water. This mindfulness practice can be applied to life's challenges, helping you remain calm and present even when faced with uncertainty.

By concentrating on the sensation of your body moving through the water and the steady pattern of your breath, you quiet the noise in your mind and gain clarity. This practice allows you to observe your thoughts without getting caught up in them, enabling you to face problems with a clear and open mind.

Incorporating swimming as a regular practice helps you develop the mental and physical resilience to handle life's waves. Just as swimming strengthens your body and improves your cardiovascular health, it also enhances your ability to cope with stress and manage emotions.

Every time you swim through the waves, you build confidence in your ability to face life's challenges with calmness and strength. The ocean becomes a metaphor for life's unpredictable nature, and by learning to swim through it, you learn how to navigate your own challenges with grace.

Coastal Stride:

Strengthen Your Body, Calm Your Mind

In a world that never seems to slow down, stress can often feel like an uninvited companion. One of the most effective ways to combat stress and regain control is through physical activity, with brisk walking being one of the simplest yet most powerful exercises available. A brisk walk not only serves as a great form of cardiovascular exercise but also acts as an opportunity to clear your mind, relieve tension, and build physical resilience. By engaging in this activity regularly, you can foster both mental and physical well-being, allowing you to cope better with life's challenges.

When you walk briskly, your body enters a state of physical exertion that helps to release tension built up from stress. As you move, your heart rate increases, blood flow improves, and your body begins to release endorphins—the natural mood boosters.

This release of stress-relieving hormones can help you feel lighter, both physically and mentally, and provide a sense of clarity. With each step, you can feel the weight of your concerns lifting as you focus on your stride, your breathing, and the rhythm of your movement. This simple yet effective activity shifts your attention away from stressors, creating a sense of relief and relaxation.

A brisk walk also offers a chance to observe how physical exertion can build resilience. As you walk at a steady pace, you challenge your body to move for an extended period of time. The more frequently you walk, the stronger and more capable your body becomes, improving endurance, stamina, and overall strength.

Similarly, this physical challenge mirrors how resilience develops in the face of life's difficulties. Just as walking becomes easier with practice, facing challenges with persistence and focus builds mental resilience. Each walk provides an opportunity to notice how your body adapts and strengthens, reminding you that stress, like physical exertion, can be overcome with consistency and effort.

In addition to physical benefits, walking can also serve as a mindful experience. While you walk, you have the chance to engage with your surroundings. Take in the sights, sounds, and smells of your environment—whether it's the rustling of leaves, the feeling of the wind on your skin, or the rhythm of your footsteps on the ground.

Mindful walking helps you stay present in the moment, shifting your focus from stress to a deeper connection with your body and your environment. This mindfulness practice strengthens your ability to manage stress in everyday life, providing mental clarity and a greater sense of well-being.

The benefits of brisk walking extend beyond the walk itself. As you begin to incorporate this activity into your daily routine, you may notice a reduction in stress levels, better physical health, and an increased sense of resilience. Regular brisk walking strengthens not only your body but also your ability to cope with the demands of life. It teaches you how to push through challenges, both physical and emotional, and develop a stronger sense of self. By embracing the power of movement, you create a foundation of health and resilience that helps you handle stress with greater ease.

From the Shoreline to Your Soul:

Journaling the Power of Movement

Incorporating physical movement into your daily routine offers not only physical benefits but also an opportunity for introspection and growth. One powerful way to enhance the experience of movement is through reflection, particularly journaling about how your body responds to exercise.

This practice can help you gain a deeper understanding of how your body feels, what challenges you encounter, and how movement empowers you to tackle difficulties with renewed energy. Journaling allows you to connect with your body's sensations and emotional responses, reinforcing the connection between physical and mental health.

When you engage in any form of exercise, whether it's walking, yoga, or swimming, your body goes through a range of sensations. From the initial warm-up to the release of endorphins after the activity, these physical changes can offer valuable insights into how stress and tension manifest in your body.

By taking a moment to write down your experiences, you can observe how your muscles feel, how your breath shifts, and any emotional responses that arise during or after the movement. For instance, you might notice that your shoulders are less tense after a walk or that your mind feels clearer after a yoga session. This awareness helps you connect your physical practice with the mental and emotional benefits it provides.

The act of journaling also creates space for you to identify and reflect on challenges you feel ready to face with renewed energy. Physical movement has a remarkable way of releasing pent-up stress and increasing your resilience. After a workout, you may feel more confident and energized, ready to take on challenges in other areas of your life.

Journaling can help you articulate these shifts, encouraging you to recognize how movement empowers you. For example, if you've been struggling with a difficult project at work or a personal goal, you might write about how your body feels stronger and more capable after exercise, and how this newfound energy can help you overcome obstacles.

Additionally, journaling about your body's responses to movement can foster a mindset of self-compassion and progress. As you reflect on your physical practice, it's important to recognize not just the triumphs but also the areas where you've experienced challenges. Perhaps a certain stretch feels difficult, or your stamina is tested during a walk.

These moments of difficulty are part of the process of growth. By acknowledging them in your journal, you give yourself the opportunity to learn from these experiences and celebrate the progress you've made. Reflecting on how far you've come strengthens your motivation to continue moving forward, both in your physical practice and in your personal life.

Finally, journaling about your body's response to movement offers an opportunity to track your progress over time. As you regularly reflect on your experiences, you may begin to notice patterns in how your body feels before and after exercise, and how these sensations relate to your emotional state.

Over weeks and months, this practice can show you how far you've come, highlighting improvements in strength, endurance, and emotional resilience. Tracking these changes not only reinforces the value of your physical activity but also encourages you to continue facing challenges with a positive, growth-oriented mindset.

Waves of Wellness:

Understanding the Impact of Movement

Exercise is an important practice that not only strengthens the body but also offers mental clarity and emotional resilience. After engaging in physical activities like walking, yoga, swimming, or stretching, it is essential to reflect on how these movements have impacted both your body and mind.

The connection between physical exertion and emotional well-being is profound, as movement creates a sense of accomplishment, relieves tension, and provides mental clarity. This process of reflection helps solidify the benefits of exercise and fosters a deeper understanding of how it impacts our daily lives.

Activity reflection offers an opportunity to evaluate how physical practice has energized you. You may notice a surge of confidence or increased energy that encourages you to take on new challenges with clarity and strength.

Regular physical movement builds resilience, both physically and emotionally, which in turn enables individuals to face challenges with a sense of capability. Whether it's a work task, a difficult conversation, or a personal goal, you may find that the energy and mental clarity gained through exercise make you more prepared to tackle obstacles with renewed enthusiasm and determination.

As you reflect on the practice, think about what challenges you now feel ready to face with new strength and clarity. Perhaps there was something that felt overwhelming before your exercise, but now, after engaging in movement, it seems more manageable.

This mental shift is an important benefit of exercise, helping you build resilience and approach difficulties with a sense of control. By continuing to practice reflection, you reinforce the positive impact of exercise on your body and mind, creating a cycle of growth that supports both your physical health and emotional well-being.

The Ocean Within:

Strengthening Your Body, Renewing Your Mind

The relationship between physical health and emotional well-being is inseparable. When we prioritize physical activity, we not only strengthen our bodies but also renew our minds and emotions. Physical movement, whether through exercise, yoga, swimming, or stretching, is vital in fostering mental clarity, emotional resilience, and stress relief. Embracing the strength of your body through consistent movement is a crucial practice for overall well-being, supporting both your physical health and emotional equilibrium.

One of the most important aspects of body renewal is the connection between physical exercise and the reduction of mental and emotional stress. When we engage in physical activity, our bodies release endorphins, the "feel-good" hormones that elevate our mood and reduce feelings of anxiety and depression.

This process also helps clear our minds by redirecting our focus toward the present moment, reducing mental clutter and stress. With a consistent practice of physical activity, your body becomes a powerful tool for emotional regulation, allowing you to navigate life's challenges with greater ease and clarity.

Strengthening the body also enhances our emotional resilience, helping us cope with stress and adversity. Regular movement builds both physical endurance and emotional stability. As we face the physical challenges of a workout, yoga practice, or even a brisk walk, we build mental fortitude, teaching ourselves that we are capable of handling discomfort and pushing through obstacles. This increased emotional resilience can be applied to daily life, enabling us to manage stress, confront difficult emotions, and stay grounded in the face of uncertainty.

To embrace your body's strength, it's essential to focus on daily practices that encourage movement and self-care. Whether through stretching, walking, swimming, or yoga, dedicating time each day to connect with your body helps maintain physical vitality while supporting mental health. Simple practices like taking deep breaths, stretching gently, or focusing on the sensation of movement can help center your mind and create a sense of calm. These practices provide a moment of peace in a busy world and help you reconnect with your body's inherent strength.

Waves of Reflection:

Embracing the Day's Lessons

As you wind down at the close of Day 3, take a moment to reflect on the power of movement in your life. Whether it's through yoga, swimming, or a simple walk, committing to regular physical activity has a way of strengthening not just the body, but the mind as well. It's in these moments of movement that we build resilience and gain clarity—tools that help us face life's challenges with confidence and grace.

Incorporating these practices into your routine doesn't just improve physical health, but it fosters emotional stability, too. Tonight, as you rest, remember that every step, stretch, and breath you take contributes to the foundation of strength and resilience you're building. Embrace the power of movement, knowing it's helping guide you toward a stronger, more resilient self. Let this thought carry you peacefully into the night, ready for whatever tomorrow brin

Day 4 ~

Waves of Joy:

Reconnecting with Nature and Creativity

Sandy Toes and Playful Souls:

Rediscover Joy Through Nature

With life pulling us in so many directions, it's easy to forget the simple joys of being in nature and allowing ourselves the freedom to play. Taking time to immerse yourself in the natural world can be a powerful antidote to stress and burnout. Nature offers a soothing escape, encouraging a connection to both the environment and our own creative spirit.

Whether it's walking barefoot on the sand, collecting shells, or simply observing the world around you, nature has the ability to reignite your sense of wonder and curiosity. By stepping away from the distractions of daily life, we allow ourselves the opportunity to rediscover joy, tap into our creativity, and experience moments of mindfulness.

Spending time outdoors reconnects us with a slower, more intentional way of being. In nature, there is no rush. The rhythm of the waves, the sway of the trees, and the soft sounds of the earth invite us to slow down and fully engage with the present moment. So, on Day 4, we will immerse ourselves in the natural world in order to get back in touch with our playful, creative selves.

This immersion helps break free from the constant mental chatter that often leaves us feeling overwhelmed. Nature becomes a canvas for exploration and creativity, whether it's through capturing a beautiful scene with a camera, creating something with found objects like seashells or leaves, or simply being inspired by the world around us.

Engaging in creative activities while immersed in nature not only stimulates your imagination but also brings out your inner playfulness. Activities like building sandcastles, sketching a scenic view, or simply exploring trails can help you tap into a more carefree and curious mindset. These moments of playful exploration allow us to experience joy without judgment or expectation.

They provide a break from structured routines and allow space for personal expression and experimentation. Creativity is not confined to traditional artistic forms—it can be found in how we interact with nature, how we see the world, and how we choose to express our thoughts and feelings.

Creativity and nature also complement each other in profound ways. Nature provides an abundant source of inspiration, whether it's the vibrant colors of the sky during sunset, the intricate patterns in a seashell, or the textures of tree bark. The very act of observing nature encourages mindfulness, helping us engage with our surroundings in a deeper way.

This connection with nature helps reduce stress, enhances mental clarity, and promotes emotional balance. By taking time to engage creatively, whether through photography, sketching, or simply collecting items, we learn to appreciate the beauty in small moments and rediscover our sense of play.

Immersing ourselves in nature and embracing creativity is not just about relaxation—it's about reawakening parts of ourselves that may have been dormant. We all have a playful, curious side, but sometimes life gets in the way.

Nature has a way of gently coaxing these parts of ourselves to the surface, reminding us of the simple joy that comes with exploring the world around us. By committing to regular time outdoors and engaging in creative activities, we not only benefit our emotional and mental well-being but also tap into a deeper, more joyful connection with life.

Tidal Flow:

Blending Nature's Calm with Creative Energy

In our busy, modern lives, it can be difficult to tap into a sense of wonder and creativity. Often, we become so consumed with routines, tasks, and responsibilities that we lose touch with the simple pleasures of play. One powerful way to reignite that sense of joy is by immersing ourselves in nature and engaging in creative activities.

This combination not only allows us to reconnect with the natural world but also invites us to rediscover our playful spirit. By stepping away from our usual environments, we give ourselves permission to be present, curious, and open to the beauty and inspiration that surrounds us.

Nature immersion has proven benefits for both mental and physical well-being. According to many scientists and psychologists, spending time in nature helps reduce stress, improve mood, and even boost cognitive function. Nature provides an environment where we can unwind, breathe deeply, and clear our minds.

At the beach, the constant rhythm of the waves, the expansive horizon, and the tactile sensation of sand beneath your feet create an ideal backdrop for mindfulness. Taking a walk along the shore, breathing in the salty air, or simply observing the ocean's ebb and flow allows you to be present in a way that feels refreshing and grounding.

While nature immersion offers physical and mental benefits, combining it with creative exploration takes the experience to another level. The beach offers a natural playground for creative activities like photography, sketching, or collecting shells. These activities encourage us to see the world through a fresh lens and engage in new forms of expression.

When we take time to create—whether through art, writing, or even play—we break free from the structured demands of our daily lives and allow ourselves to simply *be*. Creative exploration nurtures our playful side, helping us reconnect with joy and curiosity that often gets lost in the busyness of life.

One of the great advantages of combining nature immersion with creative exploration is the opportunity to embrace spontaneity. Nature doesn't require perfection, and the beach's ever-changing landscape encourages experimentation.

Whether you are building a sandcastle, collecting interesting shells, or sketching the waves as they crash, the process of creating is more important than the outcome. It's about tapping into the present moment and enjoying the act of exploration. This approach can bring us back to a childlike sense of wonder and joy, reminding us that creativity can be found in the simplest of activities.

By incorporating both nature immersion and creative exploration into your routine, you invite a sense of balance and peace into your life. Nature offers a space to breathe and reset, while creative activities provide a chance for self-expression and exploration.

Whether it's finding inspiration in the textures of rocks and shells or capturing the beauty of a sunset through photography, the opportunities for creativity are endless. Together, nature and creativity foster mindfulness and curiosity, two key ingredients for living a more fulfilled and playful life.

Waves of Awareness:

Immersing in Nature's Present Moment

Spending time in nature offers countless benefits for our mental, emotional, and physical well-being. In a world full of distractions, taking the time to fully immerse ourselves in the natural environment allows us to reconnect with both the world around us and ourselves. One of the most powerful ways to do this is by engaging in simple activities like walking barefoot in the sand, collecting shells, or sitting quietly by the waves.

These activities allow us to embrace the present moment and experience the calming effects of nature on a deeper level. In this essay, we will explore the importance of being present in nature and how these simple activities can enhance mindfulness and overall well-being.

Walking barefoot in the sand is a simple yet powerful way to connect with nature. As your feet sink into the soft sand, you are reminded of the tactile sensations of the earth beneath you, a feeling that many people overlook in their daily lives. This grounding activity can help you become more attuned to your body, allowing you to feel the temperature of the sand, the shifting textures, and the rhythmic flow of each step.

As you walk, try to focus on the sensations in your body rather than your thoughts or concerns. The act of walking barefoot encourages mindfulness by fostering a sense of presence, helping you tune out distractions and engage with your surroundings in a more profound way.

Collecting shells is another mindful activity that can deepen your connection to nature. As you stroll along the shoreline, gather seashells of different shapes, sizes, and colors. Each shell represents a unique aspect of the natural world, and by focusing on the small details of each one, you can cultivate a sense of appreciation for nature's beauty.

Collecting shells offers an opportunity for creative expression, whether you choose to create a display or simply reflect on the moment. This activity can also bring a sense of calm and focus, as it requires you to slow down and appreciate the intricate details of the environment. Through this practice, you can learn to value the small moments of life and gain a deeper sense of connection to the world around you.

Sitting quietly by the waves is one of the most powerful ways to immerse yourself in nature and tap into its soothing effects. The sound of the waves, the movement of the water, and the vastness of the ocean create a sense of peace and tranquility. By sitting in silence and simply observing the natural beauty around you, you can clear your mind and experience a deep sense of calm.

Focus on your breath as it synchronizes with the rhythm of the waves, allowing your thoughts to fade into the background. This simple act of sitting by the water helps cultivate mindfulness and encourages emotional clarity, making it a perfect practice for releasing stress and finding inner peace.

The benefits of immersing yourself in nature are vast, and the simple activities mentioned above are powerful tools for cultivating presence and mindfulness. Spending uninterrupted time in nature allows you to step away from the chaos of daily life and focus on the present moment.

Whether it's feeling the sand between your toes, collecting shells, or simply sitting by the water, each activity encourages a deeper connection to the natural world and helps you cultivate a more mindful, peaceful state of mind. Nature offers a powerful reminder to slow down, appreciate the present, and reconnect with our surroundings in a meaningful way.

Tidal Harmony:

A Sensory Journey through Nature

Mindfulness is the practice of being fully present in the moment, and one of the most effective ways to cultivate this awareness is through connecting with nature. Nature offers an abundance of sensory experiences—sight, sound, touch, and even smell—that can help us ground ourselves and tune in to our surroundings.

By fully engaging our senses while spending time outdoors, we not only enhance our connection to the natural world, but we also foster a deeper sense of mindfulness that can have lasting benefits for our mental, emotional, and physical well-being. In this essay, we will explore the benefits of engaging the senses—sight, sound, and touch—when connecting with nature, and provide easy-to-follow guidelines for incorporating mindfulness into your outdoor experiences.

The sense of sight is one of the most immediate ways to connect with nature. When you step outside, take a moment to truly look around and observe the environment. Notice the colors of the landscape, the patterns in the leaves, and the movement of the clouds in the sky. Whether you're by the beach, in the woods, or in a park, each setting offers unique visual stimuli that can encourage mindfulness.

Focusing on the details in the world around you—like the play of light on the water or the shape of tree branches—can help bring your attention to the present moment, leaving behind distractions and anxieties. By noticing the richness of your surroundings, you are not only engaging your sight but also cultivating a sense of appreciation for the beauty of nature.

Sound is another important aspect of mindfulness in nature. The sounds of nature—whether it's the crashing of ocean waves, the rustling of leaves in the wind, or the chirping of birds—can create a calming and grounding effect on the mind. These natural sounds have been shown to reduce stress and anxiety, providing a sense of peace and tranquility.

As you spend time outdoors, take a moment to close your eyes and listen intently to the sounds around you. Try to distinguish different layers of sound: the rhythm of the waves, the hum of insects, or the whisper of the breeze. By tuning in to the sounds of nature, you can quiet your mind and become more present in the moment, helping you to release tension and stress.

Touch is another powerful way to connect with nature and enhance mindfulness. Nature offers a wide range of tactile experiences, from the sensation of warm sand between your toes to the cool touch of a tree's bark. These sensations can help anchor you in the present and encourage full-body awareness.

Take time to engage your sense of touch by walking barefoot on the ground, feeling the textures of leaves or stones, or running your fingers through the grass. Each touch brings you closer to your environment and helps you become more attuned to your body and surroundings. By incorporating touch into your outdoor experience, you enhance your mindfulness practice and develop a deeper connection to the world around you.

Engaging the senses in nature also promotes relaxation and mental clarity. As you immerse yourself in the sights, sounds, and sensations of the natural world, you shift your focus away from the busyness of everyday life. This shift not only helps you become more present, but it also reduces stress and enhances emotional well-being.

Whether you're enjoying a quiet moment by the water, hiking through the woods, or simply sitting in a park, engaging with nature through your senses encourages relaxation and a deeper sense of inner peace. By regularly practicing this mindfulness connection, you can experience greater clarity, calm, and emotional resilience.

Ocean Breeze Healing:

Rebalancing Body and Mind

Spending time in nature has long been associated with numerous physical, mental, and emotional benefits. Whether it's taking a walk in the park, hiking through the woods, or simply sitting by the ocean, immersing ourselves in natural surroundings can have a profound impact on our well-being.

One of the most significant advantages of spending time outdoors is its ability to reduce stress, clear the mind, and restore a sense of balance. In this essay, we will explore how nature helps alleviate stress, promote mental clarity, and bring about a sense of emotional and physical equilibrium, while providing easy-to-follow guidelines for incorporating more nature time into your daily routine.

One of the most immediate effects of time spent in nature is its ability to reduce stress. Research has shown that being in natural environments lowers cortisol levels, the hormone associated with stress. Whether you're walking through a forest, sitting by the beach, or hiking up a mountain, nature has a calming effect on the body, lowering blood pressure and heart rate.

To take advantage of this, aim to spend at least 20 minutes a day in a natural setting. It could be as simple as a stroll through your local park, breathing in the fresh air and observing the surroundings. As you do this, notice how your body feels and pay attention to the relaxation you experience as you leave behind the pressures of daily life.

In addition to reducing stress, nature also clears the mind and enhances mental clarity. In the whirlwind of daily responsibilities, we are constantly bombarded with information and distractions that make it difficult to focus. Time in nature offers a respite from the noise, allowing the mind to reset. Natural environments have been shown to improve cognitive function, concentration, and creativity, as well as reduce mental fatigue.

To harness this benefit, try to spend some time in nature with the intention of clearing your mind. Focus on the present moment, observe the beauty around you, and let go of any mental clutter. This practice can help sharpen your thinking, improve problem-solving, and boost your overall productivity.

Another benefit of spending time in nature is its ability to restore a sense of balance and well-being. When we immerse ourselves in nature, we often experience a sense of grounding—feeling connected to something larger than ourselves. Nature provides a space for reflection, peace, and emotional healing, helping us regain a sense of harmony in our lives.

Whether it's sitting by a lake, feeling the sand between your toes, or listening to the waves crash on the shore, these moments of connection can help us recalibrate emotionally. To incorporate this into your routine, try setting aside a specific time each day or week to be outdoors. Practice mindfulness during this time, focusing on your breath and the present moment, and allow yourself to feel the restorative power of nature.

Spending time outdoors also offers numerous physical health benefits, including improved immune function, better sleep quality, and increased physical fitness. By incorporating outdoor activities into your daily life, such as walking, swimming, or cycling, you not only improve your physical health but also contribute to your overall emotional well-being.

These activities provide an opportunity to move your body while benefiting from the calming and healing properties of nature. To make the most of this, try incorporating physical activities that you enjoy into your time in nature. Whether it's hiking, yoga, or simply walking on the beach, moving your body outdoors enhances both physical and mental health.

Sands of Discovery:

Unlocking Your Creative Spirit

Creative exploration is a powerful tool for unlocking joy, curiosity, and a sense of playfulness in our lives. Engaging in creative activities allows us to tap into our imagination, express emotions, and see the world from a fresh perspective. Whether through photography, sketching, or any other form of artistic expression, creativity offers a way to reconnect with the present moment and our inner child.

One of the most significant benefits of engaging in creative expression is its ability to reduce stress and enhance emotional well-being. When we engage in creative activities, we shift our focus away from the pressures and worries of daily life. Instead of ruminating on problems or challenges, our attention becomes absorbed in the act of creation.

Whether you are capturing a beautiful scene with your camera or sketching the world around you, the process allows you to be fully present and focused on the task at hand. To incorporate this into your routine, set aside time to simply observe your surroundings and capture moments that spark your creativity. It could be the way the light hits the water, a unique shape in the sand, or a beautiful sunset—these small moments of beauty can help shift your focus from stress to joy.

Engaging in creative activities also helps to develop a deeper connection with the environment around you. When you take the time to photograph or sketch nature, you are forced to slow down and pay attention to the details that you might otherwise overlook. Creative exploration encourages mindfulness, as it requires you to be present and observant.

To deepen this connection, try to practice mindfulness while engaging in your creative activity. Whether you're snapping photos of flowers or sketching a beach scene, allow yourself to fully immerse in the process without judgment or distraction. This practice of paying attention to the world with fresh eyes can inspire a greater appreciation for nature and the present moment.

Another important benefit of creative expression is its ability to foster a sense of curiosity and playfulness. As adults, it can be easy to forget the importance of play and exploration. We often become bogged down by responsibilities and routines, losing touch with our ability to approach life with a sense of wonder. Engaging in creative activities like photography or sketching invites us to rediscover our playful side.

These activities offer a chance to experiment, make mistakes, and explore the world without any expectations or pressures. Whether you're taking a spontaneous photo of a unique shell or sketching a scene that catches your eye, creative expression encourages you to play, explore, and enjoy the process.

Creativity also fosters problem-solving and critical thinking skills, which can translate to other areas of life. When you engage in creative expression, you often encounter challenges that require you to think outside the box or approach problems in new ways. For example, capturing the perfect photograph may involve adjusting lighting, framing, and perspective. Sketching a scene may require you to focus on proportions, shading, and detail.

These problem-solving processes not only sharpen your creative skills but also enhance your ability to think critically in everyday situations. To apply this to your practice, try experimenting with different angles, lighting, and techniques in your creative exploration. Push yourself to think creatively and problem-solve as you go along.

Finally, engaging in creative activities can be deeply satisfying and rewarding. The sense of accomplishment you feel after capturing a beautiful photo or completing a sketch can boost your self-esteem and overall happiness. These moments of creative expression offer a chance to celebrate your unique perspective and abilities.

To make the most of this, try to set aside time each week to engage in a creative activity, whether it's photography, sketching, or another form of artistic expression. Keep a journal or portfolio of your work to track your progress and celebrate your creativity.

Waves of Perspective: Rediscovering Your Surroundings

Engaging in creative exercises can transform the way we experience and connect with our surroundings. By embracing activities like photography, journaling, or sketching, we open ourselves up to new perspectives and a deeper appreciation of the world around us.

These creative outlets encourage us to slow down, observe carefully, and express our unique experiences. In this essay, we'll explore how to use creativity to shift our perception of the environment and offer prompts to inspire fresh ways of seeing.

Photography is one of the most accessible and rewarding creative practices to explore when trying to see the world through a new lens. It encourages us to pay attention to detail, composition, and lighting in ways we might otherwise overlook.

To start, take a walk and bring along your camera or smartphone. As you explore, ask yourself, "What speaks to me in the landscape?" This simple prompt will guide you to notice unique aspects of nature or your surroundings that evoke emotions or capture your attention. Whether it's the texture of a tree bark, the movement of water, or a moment of sunlight filtering through leaves, photography invites you to capture the beauty and subtlety of the present moment.

Another creative outlet is journaling, which offers a reflective space to process your thoughts and observations. Writing can help deepen your connection to the environment by encouraging you to reflect on what you notice and how it makes you feel. Try starting your journal entry with a prompt like, "How can I capture the feeling of this moment?" This can help you articulate what you're experiencing, whether it's the calm of a quiet landscape or the energy of a busy street.

Journaling also allows you to explore your thoughts and emotions more deeply, fostering self-awareness and mindfulness. Consider writing down your sensory experiences—the sights, sounds, and smells of the environment—and how they contribute to the atmosphere around you.

For those who enjoy drawing or sketching, this practice can offer another way to connect creatively with your environment. Sketching is a powerful tool for observing details and translating them into art. Unlike photography, sketching encourages you to engage with the scene more intimately, requiring you to pay close attention to proportions, textures, and lines. As you sketch, consider asking yourself, "What can I bring to life on paper that I might otherwise miss?"

This prompt invites you to notice intricate patterns, colors, or movements that stand out to you. Sketching offers the freedom to interpret the world in your unique way, creating a personal connection to the landscape.

Regardless of the creative medium you choose, the key is to approach your environment with a sense of curiosity and openness. Whether it's through the lens of a camera, the pages of a journal, or the strokes of a pencil, creativity allows you to transform your surroundings into something new.

Try stepping outside your usual routines and view familiar places with fresh eyes. You may notice details you never saw before, or experience a deeper emotional connection to the spaces around you. The practice of creativity encourages you to explore and express your inner world, making the external world richer and more meaningful.

Incorporating creativity into your daily life not only allows you to connect with your surroundings but also offers a way to express your feelings, thoughts, and personal perspectives. These creative exercises can help you rediscover joy in the small details of everyday life, cultivate mindfulness, and develop a deeper sense of gratitude for the present moment. By practicing regularly, you will enhance your ability to see the world with greater clarity and openness, creating a lasting impact on both your emotional and mental well-being.

Tidal Treasures: Uncovering New Joys Through Discovery

Exploring new environments can reignite a sense of curiosity and joy, and there's no better place to do so than at a beautiful beach. Whether you're visiting a well-known coastal destination or a hidden gem, the beach offers a variety of unique features that invite exploration.

On Day 4, we'll explore the benefits of engaging in an exploration activity, focusing on discovering the beach's local trails and quaint shops. By embracing curiosity and taking time to discover the little details around you, you can reignite a playful spirit and deepen your connection to the place you're visiting.

One of the most enjoyable ways to explore the beach is by walking along local trails. Many beaches offer trails that wind through natural landscapes such as dunes, forests, or wetlands. These trails provide an opportunity to immerse yourself in the beach's environment while also offering a gentle form of exercise.

As you walk, take time to observe your surroundings. Notice the sounds of the ocean, the scent of saltwater in the air, and the way sunlight filters through the trees. The more mindful you are during your walk, the more you'll connect with the environment and notice details you might otherwise miss.

In addition to trails, quaint shops near the beach provide another exciting opportunity for exploration. These local businesses often offer unique products that reflect the culture and charm of the area. Whether it's a handmade beach-inspired necklace, locally sourced art, or organic skincare products, visiting these shops provides a way to support the local community while discovering special items.

As you explore, engage with the shopkeepers and ask about their products and stories. These interactions help deepen your understanding of the place and connect you to the people who live there. Exploring shops can also spark new ideas for creative projects or even inspire a new hobby.

Exploration is also an opportunity to tap into your sense of curiosity. When you step into a new place, your mind opens up to the possibilities of discovery. A simple walk or a visit to a new store can reveal hidden gems, from a secret beach cove to a local restaurant with the best seafood.

Allow yourself to wander without a specific agenda, and be open to whatever you might encounter. This spontaneous approach encourages a playful mindset, helping you break free from routines and experience the joy of discovery.

Taking time to explore also cultivates mindfulness and presence. In our busy lives, it's easy to overlook the beauty around us, but when we make an effort to explore, we train ourselves to pay attention to the present moment. Whether you're admiring the view from a coastal trail or finding a unique item in a local shop, exploration encourages you to engage with your surroundings in a way that feels fresh and exciting. This simple act of discovering something new can be deeply satisfying and remind you of the joy that can come from engaging with the world around you.

Ocean Breeze Moments:

Finding Personal Inspiration on the Horizon

Exploring new places and immersing yourself in different environments can unlock creative ideas and spark deep reflections. Whether you're strolling along a beach, hiking through local trails, or browsing unique shops, these experiences can serve as a powerful source of inspiration.

By fostering a personal connection with your surroundings, you allow your mind and spirit to open up to new perspectives and creative possibilities. The very act of exploration can inspire creativity and personal reflection, and offer guidelines on how to connect deeply with your environment to enhance your creative process.

The first step in fostering a personal connection during your exploration is to approach each moment with curiosity and openness. When you walk along a beach or visit a new place, don't rush. Take time to observe, listen, and absorb the details around you. Notice the colors, textures, and patterns that surround you, as well as the sounds, smells, and feelings these moments evoke.

By slowing down and engaging all your senses, you create a foundation for inspiration to emerge. Whether you are admiring the waves crashing on the shore or pausing to appreciate the quiet of a wooded trail, allowing yourself to be present can spark a new sense of creativity.

Another way to connect with your environment is by reflecting on how it makes you feel. After exploring a new trail or visiting a local shop, take a moment to journal about your experience. Write down your thoughts, feelings, and any ideas that come to mind. Was there something about the landscape that moved you? Did a particular conversation with a shopkeeper or the discovery of a unique item ignite a new creative thought?

These reflections not only deepen your connection with the place but also offer a well of inspiration for future projects. Writing down your thoughts helps capture fleeting moments of creativity before they slip away, allowing you to revisit them later when you need new ideas.

Engaging in creative activities during your exploration can also help strengthen the personal connection you're developing with your surroundings. For example, sketching the landscape or taking photographs can help you translate the beauty of your environment into a creative expression.

These activities force you to pay close attention to details, and by doing so, you begin to notice aspects of the environment that you might otherwise overlook. The simple act of drawing or capturing an image can deepen your connection with the scene, and provide a visual record of your creative inspiration.

It's important to remember that the creative ideas you gain from exploration don't have to be huge or groundbreaking. Sometimes, the smallest moments can lead to the most profound reflections or ideas. Perhaps the texture of a seashell reminds you of an unfinished project, or a fleeting interaction with a local vendor sparks a story for your next creative piece.

The key is to allow yourself the freedom to explore without judgment or expectation, and to be open to whatever thoughts or inspirations arise along the way. Each moment, no matter how small, can hold the seed for new creative endeavors.

Finally, allow yourself to revisit your explorations regularly. Creativity, like any skill, benefits from consistent practice. By continuing to engage with your environment and reflect on your experiences, you'll nurture a deeper and more authentic creative process.

Whether it's through journaling, sketching, or simply paying attention to the world around you, each exploration will contribute to your growth as both an artist and a person. The more you connect with your environment, the more it will inspire your creativity.

Waves of Creation:

Crafting Inspired by the Sea

Creativity is not just about producing something beautiful or finished—it's about engaging with the world in a way that taps into our imagination and feelings. A powerful way to foster creativity is by creating something inspired by the experiences of the day, especially when those experiences are rooted in nature.

Whether it's a piece of art, a photo journal, a written reflection, or even something playful like a sandcastle, taking time to express yourself creatively helps solidify the connection between your inner world and the environment. Let's explore how you can turn your day spent in nature into a creative expression and provide easy-to-follow guidelines for the process.

The first step is to reflect on your day and the moments that stood out. As you spend time outdoors, whether you're walking along a beach, hiking through the woods, or simply sitting under a tree, there will be particular moments or elements that grab your attention. It could be the way the light filters through the leaves, the texture of the sand beneath your feet, or the feeling of the wind on your face. Take a few moments to consider what resonated with you. Did you notice the colors, sounds, or smells that made the moment special? Use these sensory details as the foundation for your creative project.

Once you have your inspiration, choose the medium that feels most natural to you. If you enjoy visual art, consider sketching or painting a scene that captured your attention. A photograph might also be a great way to freeze the moment in time. If you prefer writing, a short reflection or poem can help capture the essence of the experience.

Sometimes, the act of creating can be as simple as gathering natural materials like shells or stones and arranging them in a way that reflects your connection to the place. Whatever medium you choose, allow the creative process to be fluid and spontaneous, letting the inspiration from your day guide you.

Next, engage in the creative process without worrying about perfection. The goal is not to create a polished piece of work, but to immerse yourself in the act of making. If you're building a sandcastle, for example, let the sand be shaped in a way that reflects your mood and the environment—whether it's a towering castle or a simple mound.

If you're taking photos, let the lens capture the emotion of the moment rather than focusing on technical perfection. By removing the pressure of creating something "perfect," you free yourself to explore and express your feelings and experiences more authentically.

Be sure to take a moment to reflect on the creative process after you've finished. Whether it's reviewing your photo journal, looking at your art piece, or reading over your written reflection, think about how your creation reflects your experience in nature.

How did the act of creating deepen your connection to the environment? Did the creative process help you see the world around you in a new way? Allowing yourself to reflect on the act of creation can enhance your appreciation for the time spent outdoors and encourage a deeper sense of connection to your surroundings.

Shoreline Reflections: Deepening Connections Through Creative Expression

Creative expression is a powerful tool that not only allows us to share our feelings and experiences but also helps us connect more deeply with our inner selves. Whether through art, writing, music, or other forms of creativity, the process of creating something uniquely personal allows for self-reflection and emotional growth.

Creative expression helps deepen our emotional connection to experiences by allowing us to process and make sense of them. When we engage in a creative activity, we often find that we connect with our emotions in a way that might not be possible through other means. For example, a painting or a poem might allow us to capture feelings that are difficult to articulate with words alone.

Through creativity, we can explore our thoughts and emotions in a safe and structured way, leading to a better understanding of ourselves and the world around us. By expressing our emotions through creativity, we often find that we feel more connected to those feelings, and as a result, we deepen our connection to the experiences that inspired them.

Additionally, creativity provides a channel for personal reflection. When we create, we are not only expressing our emotions but also examining them from different perspectives. Whether we're journaling, drawing, or making music, the act of creation often sparks moments of introspection.

As we reflect on our work, we may notice patterns in our thoughts or begin to understand unresolved feelings. This process of reflection helps us grow emotionally and mentally, providing clarity and insight into aspects of our lives we may not have fully understood before. Creative expression becomes a tool for personal discovery, helping us connect the dots between our experiences and our emotional responses.

It's also important to note that creativity doesn't need to be about creating something perfect. The focus should be on the enjoyment of the process itself. Too often, people are discouraged from being creative because they feel their work isn't good enough.

However, creativity is not about perfection—it's about expressing what we feel in the moment and allowing ourselves to explore without judgment.

Whether we create something that looks like a masterpiece or simply enjoy the act of creating, the value lies in the freedom and self-expression it provides. Embracing the process and not worrying about the outcome allows for greater personal liberation and encourages us to continue exploring our creative abilities.

Engaging in creative activities can help reduce stress and increase emotional resilience. When we immerse ourselves in a creative endeavor, our minds focus on the present moment. This mindfulness aspect of creativity helps clear away worries and distractions, allowing us to feel more centered and calm.

As we engage in the process of creation, we often experience a sense of flow—a mental state where we are fully absorbed in the task at hand. This state of flow not only helps us reduce anxiety but also strengthens our ability to cope with challenges in other areas of life, as we build emotional resilience through creative expression.

Ocean Breezes and Creative Seas:

Embracing Joy Every Day

In our busy lives, it's easy to forget the importance of joy, playfulness, and creativity. These elements, however, are essential for maintaining a healthy, balanced, and fulfilling life. One of the most accessible ways to nurture these qualities is through immersion in nature and engaging in creative activities.

Whether it's spending time outdoors, exploring your surroundings, or expressing yourself through art or writing, these activities can reignite a sense of wonder and provide a much-needed escape from daily stresses. By incorporating nature immersion and creativity into your everyday routine, you can cultivate mindfulness and joy, improving your overall well-being.

Spending time in nature offers numerous physical and mental health benefits. Walking barefoot in the sand, sitting by the waves, or simply breathing in the fresh air can reduce stress, increase focus, and restore a sense of balance. Nature provides a serene and calming environment that encourages mindfulness, helping to clear the mind and allow for deeper emotional connections.

Whether you're taking a short walk, exploring nature trails, or simply sitting outside, these moments of immersion in the natural world can have a lasting positive impact on your mood and overall mental health. By making these small moments a part of your daily life, you nurture a deeper connection to the environment and yourself.

Creativity is another powerful tool for fostering joy and playfulness. Engaging in creative activities, such as photography, journaling, or sketching, helps you tap into your imagination and explore the world around you with fresh eyes. Creativity encourages curiosity and invites you to express emotions, ideas, and experiences in unique ways.

Whether you're capturing a moment in nature or creating something inspired by your surroundings, the act of creating brings a sense of accomplishment and fulfillment. Additionally, creative expression provides an outlet for processing thoughts and emotions, offering clarity and insight into your inner world.

Incorporating creativity into your daily routine doesn't require perfection—it's about the process. Whether you're building a sandcastle, journaling your thoughts, or creating a simple piece of art, the focus should be on expressing yourself freely without concern for the outcome. Engaging in creative activities in a playful, relaxed manner allows you to experience joy in the moment, helping to alleviate stress and create a sense of well-being.

As you explore new ways of seeing your environment, you also open yourself up to new ideas and possibilities, further enhancing your connection to the world around you. When combined, nature immersion and creativity provide an enriching experience that promotes mindfulness, emotional balance, and joy.

These activities foster a sense of wonder and encourage you to be present in the moment, reminding you of the beauty and potential in everyday life. By making time for nature and creative expression, you can create a life that feels more vibrant and fulfilling. These practices nurture a playful and curious mindset, helping you embrace challenges with resilience and enthusiasm.

Ocean's Embrace:

Reflecting on a Day of Play and Peace

As we end our day, we can reflect on how nature has provided a peaceful retreat from the chaos of life, while also sparking our creativity and playful spirit. Whether through a relaxing walk, a moment of mindfulness by the water, or engaging in creative activities like photography or sketching, nature has a unique ability to restore balance, clear the mind, and reconnect us with ourselves. Creative exploration encourages us to rediscover joy, curiosity, and playfulness, enhancing emotional well-being and fostering a deeper connection with the world around us.

By embracing these moments of creativity and fun, we slow down, focus on the present, and appreciate the beauty of the world in new ways. As you close your day, take pride in the joy and creativity you embraced today, knowing that you've nurtured both your body and spirit. Let this sense of playfulness and wonder carry you into a restful sleep, rejuvenated and ready for tomorrow.

Day 5 ~

Sands of Stillness:

Resting and Reconnecting with Gratitude

Ocean of Gratitude:

Resting and Reconnecting with the Week's Blessings

Throughout our busy lives, it can be easy to overlook the moments of peace, joy, and connection that bring us true fulfillment. Taking time to reflect on these moments is an essential practice for cultivating gratitude and emotional well-being. By intentionally focusing on the blessings we've experienced, we can deepen our appreciation for the small and significant things that make life meaningful.

The combination of gratitude, rest, and connection forms a powerful foundation for emotional health, helping us recharge, appreciate life, and strengthen our relationships. On Day 5, we'll explore how recognizing these blessings can foster a sense of peace and contentment, and how integrating them into our daily lives can promote long-term well-being.

Gratitude is a simple yet profound practice that invites us to pause and appreciate the good things in our lives. By reflecting on moments that brought us joy or peace during the week, we begin to shift our mindset from one of scarcity to one of abundance. Instead of focusing on what we lack or what went wrong, we start to notice and celebrate the things that have gone right.

Whether it's a kind word from a friend, a quiet moment of reflection by the beach, or a feeling of contentment after completing a task, acknowledging these blessings can significantly impact our emotional state. As we practice gratitude, we create a habit of focusing on the positive aspects of our lives, which helps us feel more grounded and connected to our surroundings.

Rest is another vital component of this practice. In our fast-paced world, rest is often undervalued or overlooked, but it plays an essential role in rejuvenating our bodies and minds. Taking time to rest allows us to recharge our energy, improve focus, and reset emotionally. Practices like deep breathing, meditation, or simply taking a moment to sit in silence can help us restore balance.

By acknowledging the importance of rest and intentionally carving out time for it, we allow ourselves to truly disconnect from the demands of daily life and reconnect with our inner selves. Rest isn't just about sleep; it's about finding moments of stillness to refresh and rejuvenate.

Connection with others is equally important for our emotional well-being. Whether it's sharing a meaningful experience with family, friends, or even strangers, these moments of connection help us feel supported and seen. Meaningful connections bring a sense of belonging and comfort, reminding us that we are not alone in our experiences.

Sharing our joys, challenges, and gratitude with others strengthens these bonds, fostering empathy and understanding. It's in these connections that we often find solace, encouragement, and motivation. Reflecting on the people who have impacted our lives during the week can help us cultivate a deeper appreciation for the relationships we cherish.

Finally, combining gratitude, rest, and connection can create a powerful cycle of positivity and well-being. When we make time for each of these practices, we begin to notice how they support one another. Gratitude enhances our connection to others by fostering a spirit of appreciation, while rest allows us the clarity and peace to engage in meaningful reflection.

Connection, in turn, reinforces our gratitude by reminding us of the love and support that surrounds us. These elements work together to nourish our emotional health, create resilience, and promote a sense of peace in our everyday lives.

So today on Day 5, taking the time to reflect on the blessings we've experienced throughout the week—through gratitude, rest, and connection—can have profound benefits for our emotional well-being. By consciously acknowledging moments of peace and joy, we begin to shift our mindset towards positivity and appreciation.

Incorporating rest and mindful reflection into our lives allows us to recharge, while deepening our connections with others fosters a sense of belonging and support. Embracing these practices regularly can lead to a more fulfilling, balanced life, helping us navigate both the quiet moments and the challenges with grace and resilience. By making gratitude, rest, and connection a priority, we empower ourselves to embrace life with a deeper sense of peace and joy.

Tides of Tranquility: Rest and Gratitude for Emotional Balance

As we navigate the demands of our busy lives, it can be easy to overlook the importance of rest and reflection. These demands of work, family, and daily responsibilities often leave little room for us to pause and appreciate the blessings in our lives. However, taking time to reflect on the week's experiences and integrating gratitude with moments of rest can be a powerful tool for improving emotional well-being.

By slowing down and acknowledging the positive aspects of our lives, we can calm our minds, reduce stress, and foster a deeper sense of peace. This practice of rest and gratitude invites us to reflect on the moments of joy and calm that we may have taken for granted, helping us feel more centered and connected.

Gratitude is an essential practice for nurturing emotional well-being. When we actively recognize and express thankfulness for the positive experiences and people in our lives, we shift our focus away from what is lacking and instead direct our attention to what we already have.

Whether it's a moment of calm by the ocean, a meaningful conversation with a friend, or a simple act of kindness, these moments of gratitude help build resilience and foster a sense of contentment. Reflecting on the past week gives us the opportunity to pinpoint these moments and deepen our appreciation for them, strengthening our emotional foundation and reminding us of life's blessings.

Incorporating rest into this practice allows us to fully absorb the benefits of gratitude. Rest is not just about physical relaxation but also about mental and emotional rejuvenation. Taking time to slow down—whether by engaging in mindful breathing, sitting quietly, or spending time in nature—helps to calm the nervous system and promote relaxation.

This allows us to be more present and mindful, enhancing our ability to experience gratitude fully. When combined, rest and gratitude can work together to reduce stress, enhance mental clarity, and foster a sense of well-being. Taking time to reconnect with your inner peace through these practices can be incredibly restorative.

An effective way to reflect on the week's blessings is through an activity that encourages slowing down and being present. This might involve a quiet morning by the beach, where you focus on the sounds of the waves, the sensation of the sand beneath your feet, and the calm of the environment.

Another way to practice gratitude and rest is through journaling—writing down three things you're grateful for and allowing yourself to savor the peace that comes with each reflection. You can also engage in a restorative breathing exercise to center yourself, helping to clear your mind and foster a deeper connection to your own sense of peace.

The combination of rest and gratitude creates a powerful practice for reconnecting with your inner self. By reflecting on the blessings of the week, taking moments to rest, and engaging in mindful gratitude practices, you nurture your emotional well-being and cultivate a sense of peace.

These practices help to calm your mind and encourage a balanced perspective, allowing you to approach life with a greater sense of clarity and calm. As you continue to integrate rest and gratitude into your daily life, you will find that these moments of reflection not only enhance your emotional resilience but also bring a deeper sense of joy and fulfillment.

Waves of Calm:

Deep Breathing for Rest and Reflection

It's easy to feel overwhelmed by the constant demands of daily life. Our minds race from task to task, and our bodies are often tense as we try to keep up. One powerful tool to combat this stress and promote relaxation is deep, slow breathing. Deep breathing exercises help to calm the nervous system, allowing the body and mind to reset. By integrating a deep breathing practice into your daily routine, you can create a moment of stillness and mindfulness, which is essential for emotional and physical well-being.

To begin the deep breathing practice, find a peaceful environment where you won't be disturbed. This could be in a quiet room, outside in nature, or even by the beach. The setting is important because it helps to create a space where you can fully focus on your breath without distractions. Once you're settled, begin by sitting or lying down in a comfortable position. Close your eyes and take a few moments to relax your body. Pay attention to any areas of tension, and consciously release them, allowing yourself to settle into the space.

The deep breathing practice itself involves slow, controlled inhalations and exhalations. Inhale deeply through your nose for a count of four, allowing your lungs to fill completely. Hold your breath for a count of four, and then slowly exhale through your mouth for a count of six. Repeat this cycle for five to ten minutes, focusing solely on the rhythm of your breath.

As you practice, try to release any thoughts or worries that come to mind. If your mind begins to wander, gently bring your focus back to your breathing. This simple practice can help to calm the nervous system, lower heart rate, and create a sense of inner peace.

While engaging in deep breathing, it's also beneficial to incorporate reflection into the practice. As you calm your mind, take a moment to reflect on the present moment. Think about the things you're grateful for or the positive experiences from your day. You might also use this time to think about any challenges you're facing and how you might approach them with a clear, calm mind.

Reflection, paired with deep breathing, enhances the sense of mindfulness and helps create a deeper connection to yourself. It allows you to acknowledge both the joys and struggles of life with a balanced perspective, promoting emotional well-being.

Incorporating deep breathing and reflection into your daily routine can lead to significant benefits for both your mental and physical health. Not only does deep breathing calm the nervous system and reduce stress, but it also promotes mindfulness, helping you to stay present and grounded.

Over time, this practice can help you develop greater emotional resilience, as it gives you the tools to remain calm and centered in stressful situations. The combination of rest and reflection is a powerful way to nurture your well-being and build a deeper sense of peace and clarity in your life.

Seabreeze Journaling:

Embracing Gratitude Through Writing

In the hustle of daily life, we often miss the small blessings that are always around us. One effective way to foster a sense of contentment and emotional balance is through the practice of gratitude. Gratitude helps shift our focus from what we lack to what we have, cultivating a positive mindset and improving overall well-being.

By taking a few minutes each day to write down things you're grateful for, you can deepen your appreciation for the present moment and create a habit of recognizing the good in your life. The simple act of writing it down can bring clarity and peace of mind, making gratitude more tangible and accessible.

To begin your gratitude practice, find a quiet and comfortable space where you can relax and focus without distractions. It could be your favorite chair, a cozy nook by the window, or a peaceful outdoor spot. The key is to create an environment where you feel comfortable and free from interruptions.

Once settled, take a few deep breaths to center yourself and calm your mind. This moment of quiet reflection will help you tune into your thoughts and emotions, preparing you to focus on the positive aspects of your life.

After you've taken a moment to center yourself, write down three things you're grateful for. These could be small, everyday moments like a warm cup of coffee in the morning, a smile from a friend, or a beautiful sunset. They could also be more significant events, such as a promotion at work, the support of a loved one, or a personal achievement.

The key is to focus on the positive aspects of your life, no matter how big or small. There's no right or wrong answer here—gratitude is about acknowledging what brings you joy and peace in your life, and every experience holds value.

When writing, don't worry about perfect wording or lengthy explanations. Just let the words flow naturally as you reflect on the things you are thankful for. Take a moment to savor each item on your list, allowing yourself to feel the warmth and appreciation these moments bring.

Writing about your gratitude engages both your mind and body in the practice, making it easier to internalize the feelings of thankfulness. Over time, this simple habit can help retrain your mind to notice and appreciate more of the good things around you, reinforcing a positive outlook on life.

Incorporating a daily gratitude practice into your routine can have profound effects on your emotional and mental health. Research has shown that regularly expressing gratitude can reduce stress, improve mood, and even boost immune function.

By making gratitude a habit, you train your mind to focus on the positive, which can increase your overall resilience in facing life's challenges. Writing down three things you're grateful for is a simple yet powerful way to bring mindfulness and appreciation into your day, creating a more balanced and joyful mindset.

Message in a Bottle:

Writing a Gratitude Note to Yourself

Gratitude is a powerful tool for fostering emotional well-being and strengthening our resilience. Taking the time to reflect on our experiences, especially in moments of growth and challenge, allows us to appreciate our own efforts and celebrate our progress.

One of the most meaningful ways to practice gratitude is by writing a letter to yourself, thanking yourself for the strength, growth, and resilience you have shown. This exercise is a personal reflection, and there is no right or wrong way to do it. The key is to let the words flow from the heart, acknowledging your journey and honoring the person you are becoming.

To begin, find a quiet space where you feel comfortable and free from distractions. Whether it's in a peaceful corner of your home, at a cozy café, or sitting outside, choose an environment that allows you to relax and focus. Take a few deep breaths, grounding yourself in the present moment. Set your intention to write with honesty and compassion, giving yourself permission to acknowledge both the challenges and the triumphs you've experienced. This letter is for you, so be kind and generous with your words.

Start by writing down your thoughts of gratitude. Reflect on the week or a specific period in your life where you've experienced growth, strength, or resilience. Think about the moments that made you proud, the obstacles you've overcome, and the inner strength that has carried you through difficult times. You might write about how you've faced challenges with grace, how you've grown through adversity, or how you've made progress in areas that once felt impossible. Acknowledge the efforts you've put in, and recognize the courage it took to keep moving forward.

While writing, allow yourself to feel the emotions that arise. Let the words come naturally, without judgment or hesitation. This letter is meant to affirm your worth and to celebrate your journey, so don't hold back in expressing the gratitude you feel for yourself.

Even if it feels awkward at first, remember that this practice is about self-compassion and personal reflection. Take your time with it, and allow yourself to savor the moment of appreciation you are offering yourself.

Once your letter is written, read it aloud to yourself if you feel comfortable. Let the words sink in and reflect on the power of your own strength and resilience. This exercise is a reminder that you are worthy of gratitude and that the journey you are on is meaningful. By taking the time to express your appreciation for yourself, you can deepen your sense of self-compassion and enhance your emotional well-being, empowering you to face future challenges with confidence and clarity.

Sands of Kindness:

Building Connections Through Gratitude

Gratitude is not only a personal practice but also a powerful way to strengthen our connections with others. Sharing moments of joy, peace, or appreciation with friends, family, or even acquaintances deepens our relationships and fosters a sense of mutual respect and emotional support.

When we express gratitude, we create an environment of positivity that can uplift both ourselves and those around us. Taking the time to reach out and share a moment of gratitude can enhance our emotional connections and remind us of the importance of community in our lives.

To begin, think about the people in your life who have been important to you recently. This might be a close friend who has supported you through a difficult time, a family member with whom you've shared meaningful moments, or even someone you met during a trip who made an impression on you.

Reach out to them with the intention of sharing something positive—perhaps a moment of joy, peace, or a simple experience that has brought you gratitude. This act of sharing not only strengthens your bond but also spreads positive energy, creating a ripple effect of goodwill.

The next step is to choose the best way to reach out. You could send a thoughtful message, make a phone call, or even write a letter. The medium doesn't matter as much as the intention behind it. Start by sharing a specific moment or experience that made you feel grateful. It could be something as simple as a peaceful walk in nature, a kind gesture someone showed you, or an inspiring conversation you had with someone.

Be open and authentic in your sharing, allowing the recipient to feel your genuine appreciation. This act of vulnerability and openness is what deepens connections and makes gratitude feel personal.

While sharing your moment of gratitude, take the time to also express your appreciation for the connection you have with the person you're reaching out to. Let them know how much their presence, kindness, or support means to you. For example, you might say, "I'm so grateful for our conversation last week—it really helped me see things in a new light," or "I've been thinking about how much I appreciate having you in my life."

This simple expression of thanks can strengthen your relationship and create a deeper sense of connection, reminding both of you of the value of the relationship. And, as you share your gratitude, be open to receiving it in return. Gratitude is a two-way street, and often, when we express our thanks to others, it encourages them to do the same.

This exchange can leave you feeling more connected and supported, reinforcing the bonds of friendship, family, or even casual acquaintances. Sharing gratitude in this way helps create a cycle of appreciation that enhances your emotional well-being and strengthens the ties between you and others.

Calm Seas Ahead:

A Moment of Peace to Recharge and Appreciate

Amid the constant buzz of modern life, we often find ourselves overwhelmed, rushing from one task to the next, with little time for rest or reflection. However, rest is not only essential for our physical health; it also plays a crucial role in our emotional and mental well-being. Taking the time to rest allows us to recharge and restore balance in our lives. When we combine rest with gratitude, we create a powerful practice that nurtures both the mind and body. Reflecting on the peace that comes with rest and focusing on the blessings in our lives can help us cultivate a sense of calm and connection to the present moment.

To begin, find a peaceful spot that calms you. This could be by the ocean, where the rhythmic sound of the waves helps soothe your mind, or in a quiet room that feels safe and relaxing. The goal is to choose a space that feels comforting and allows you to fully embrace the moment. Once you've found your spot, take a few deep breaths, focusing on each inhale and exhale. Feel the sensation of the air entering your body and leaving it, allowing yourself to settle into the space.

As you breathe deeply, reflect on how rest and gratitude are interwoven. Rest is not just physical; it's emotional and mental. True rest involves slowing down the mind and allowing yourself to fully be present in the moment. This practice helps calm the nervous system, reduce stress, and promote a sense of peace. While resting, take a moment to recognize the gratitude you feel for the opportunity to rest and recharge. Gratitude helps us see the positive aspects of life and appreciate the simple moments that bring us joy and contentment.

Next, focus on the peace that the moment brings. Let go of any lingering thoughts or distractions and simply savor the stillness. Whether you're listening to the sound of the waves crashing, enjoying the quiet of a room, or simply observing the world around you, allow yourself to fully experience the peace in that moment. Pay attention to how it feels—what emotions rise up, what sensations you notice, and how your body responds to the calmness.

Rest, when combined with gratitude, creates a powerful opportunity for mental, emotional, and physical healing. It allows us to recharge, reflect, and reset, helping us approach life's challenges with a renewed sense of energy and perspective. By making time for rest and focusing on the blessings in our lives, we can cultivate a deep sense of well-being and resilience, allowing us to navigate life with greater ease and peace.

Sands of Serenity:

Ending the Day with Gratitude and Rest

Throughout the course of this day, we have explored the essential practices of gratitude, rest, and connection, each serving as a cornerstone for emotional and physical well-being. By integrating these practices into our daily lives, we create a foundation for peace and balance, allowing ourselves to be present and fully engage with the world around us. Gratitude shifts our focus towards positivity and contentment, while rest allows the body and mind to recharge. Together, these practices offer a powerful means of nurturing our inner peace and enhancing our overall sense of well-being.

One of the most profound aspects of today's practice is the realization that rest is not just about physical relaxation, but a holistic approach that encompasses mental and emotional rejuvenation. When we allow ourselves the space to rest and reflect, we give our minds the opportunity to process, reset, and heal. Gratitude complements this process by redirecting our thoughts towards the positive aspects of our lives, further promoting emotional balance and mental clarity.

By dedicating time to express gratitude and embrace moments of rest, we can improve our resilience to life's challenges. Regular practice of these principles fosters a sense of calm that helps us navigate the ups and downs of daily life with greater ease. As we incorporate these practices into our routine, we are reminded that both rest and gratitude are not luxury items but necessary elements of a healthy and fulfilling life.

Connection is the final piece of this trio, reminding us that our well-being is deeply intertwined with the relationships we nurture. Whether through sharing gratitude with others or simply enjoying a quiet moment in solitude, connection adds meaning to our lives. Strengthening our bonds with others and ourselves creates an environment where rest and gratitude can truly flourish.

One of the most valuable insights from today's reflection is the importance of consistency. While it may be tempting to neglect these practices in the busyness of daily life, making time for rest, gratitude, and connection regularly can significantly improve our mental and physical health. Just as we nourish our bodies with food, we must also nourish our minds and spirits with moments of quiet reflection and deep connection. By doing so, we reinforce our emotional resilience and enhance our ability to face challenges with a clear mind and a calm heart.

Incorporating these practices into our routine doesn't require grand gestures. Simple acts, such taking a few moments each day to reflect on what we are grateful for, carving out time for quiet rest, or reaching out to connect with someone, can have a profound impact on our well-being.

The first step in carrying forward the practice of rest and gratitude is to consciously carve out time each day for both. It doesn't require long periods of time; even a few minutes dedicated to quiet rest can make a significant difference.

Whether you take a short break during a busy workday to close your eyes and breathe deeply or find a quiet space to reflect on what you are grateful for, these moments of intentional pause allow you to reset and recharge. Start small by setting aside five to ten minutes each day for rest and reflection.

Next, it's important to integrate gratitude into your daily mindset. This can be as simple as taking a moment each morning to acknowledge what you're thankful for or jotting down a few thoughts in a gratitude journal each night.

Gratitude shifts our focus from what's lacking to what's abundant in our lives, helping us foster a sense of appreciation and contentment. By focusing on the positive, we can reframe challenges and gain perspective, which makes them easier to handle with a sense of calm and clarity.

Another key aspect of integrating rest and gratitude is learning to be mindful throughout the day. Even in moments of stress or busyness, pause and take a deep breath, allowing yourself to reconnect with your sense of peace. Practicing mindfulness can help you remain present and grounded, making it easier to navigate both calm and challenging moments.

Remember that rest isn't just about physical relaxation—it's also about giving your mind and spirit the space to rejuvenate. Gratitude, on the other hand, offers a mental reset that allows us to appreciate the small joys and blessings that might otherwise be overlooked.

By regularly practicing rest and gratitude, we equip ourselves with the tools to face any situation with resilience and peace. Whether in moments of tranquility or difficulty, these practices help us stay grounded, present, and emotionally balanced.

As we continue to integrate rest and gratitude into our lives, we build a strong foundation for emotional well-being that will support us through both calm and challenging times. So, as Day 5 draws to a peaceful end, take a moment tonight to rest, reflect, and be grateful—knowing that these simple acts can lead to lasting peace and a greater sense of fulfillment.

Day 6 ~

Bon Voyage:

Sailing Home with Purpose

Harboring Serenity:

Taking Calm Waters Home

When we prepare to leave a place that has brought us peace, rest, and joy, it is important to recognize that departure is not just about physically leaving a location—it is about taking the experience with us and carrying the calm, joy, and renewed perspective into our everyday lives. Now, at the close of our journey, Day 6 will ensure that we bring the tranquility of the beach back with us.

Leaving with intention allows us to transition with mindfulness, ensuring that the benefits of our time away continue to support our well-being after we return home. This approach encourages us to leave behind the chaos of everyday life and create space for peace, calm, and intentional living wherever we go.

The idea of leaving with intention begins with understanding that the energy and mindset cultivated during a retreat or reset do not have to end with the departure from that place. Instead, we can integrate the peacefulness we've experienced into our daily routine. This requires conscious reflection, creating meaningful habits, and setting an intention to stay grounded.

By making a commitment to ourselves to continue nurturing our well-being, we can bring home not just physical mementos, but a new way of thinking and being that prioritizes calm and peace in the face of life's inevitable stresses.

One powerful way to carry this peace forward is by setting a "beach mindset" habit. This habit involves identifying a practice from the retreat—such as quiet reflection, mindful breathing, or enjoying nature—and bringing it home.

For example, taking a moment each morning to enjoy a quiet cup of coffee or committing to a daily walk can help you start your day with intention and calm. These small, intentional habits can serve as anchors to remind you of the tranquility you experienced and offer you moments to reset amidst the busyness of daily life.

Another helpful practice is to create a physical reminder of the peace you've gained during your time away. Whether it's a shell from the beach, a photograph of a meaningful place, or any small memento, having a token allows you to physically connect with the emotions and experiences of your retreat.

This object can serve as a touchstone, a reminder that the peace you cultivated is always available to you. By keeping it in a visible spot, you create a constant, gentle reminder to stay grounded and intentional, even in the most hectic moments.

In addition to these practices, writing a "promise to yourself" can solidify your intention to carry peace and joy into your daily life. This promise can be as simple as committing to take time for self-care, engage in mindfulness, or prioritize moments of rest throughout the day.

Writing it down allows you to hold yourself accountable and provides a written reminder of your intention to nurture your emotional well-being. It's an easy yet powerful way to close your time away and begin the transition back to your everyday life with clarity and focus.

Sunkissed Thoughts:

Reflecting on Your Journey by the Sea

As our journey comes to a close, it's important to pause and reflect on the experiences that helped you feel calm, centered, and renewed. A key part of this reflection is considering how you can maintain the sense of peace and balance you've cultivated during your time away as you transition back into your everyday life.

It's not just about remembering the relaxation or joy you felt; it's about actively planning to carry that calm with you, integrating it into your daily routine, and making a conscious decision to maintain the sense of well-being that you've nurtured. This transition requires intention, mindfulness, and a commitment to yourself.

Start by taking a moment to reflect on what brought you peace during your time away. Was it the natural beauty of your surroundings? The simple act of slowing down? The ability to disconnect from the usual distractions and reconnect with yourself? Identify the key moments or practices that made you feel the most at ease and energized. This could include walking by the ocean, meditating, journaling, or even spending quality time with loved ones.

Once you've pinpointed what brought you peace, think about how you can bring those experiences into your everyday life. The goal is to create a routine that fosters the same sense of calm, even when you're back in the hustle and bustle of daily life.

Next, consider creating a habit or ritual that you can carry forward. This might include something as simple as starting each day with a moment of mindfulness or a quiet cup of tea, or setting aside time each week to enjoy nature or engage in a favorite creative practice. The key is consistency.

Choose one or two habits that help you reconnect with the sense of calm you experienced during your time away. Incorporate these habits into your daily life in a way that feels sustainable and meaningful to you. These small practices will serve as daily reminders to stay grounded and intentional, even on the busiest days.

In addition to creating habits, it can be helpful to keep a tangible reminder of your time away. Whether it's a photograph, a special keepsake, or even a piece of nature like a shell or stone, having a physical object that symbolizes your time away can serve as a constant reminder to return to the sense of peace you cultivated.

Place this object somewhere visible, like on your desk or nightstand, where it will gently prompt you to stay focused on maintaining your sense of calm. It will act as an anchor during stressful moments, helping you reconnect with the serenity you experienced.

Finally, make a personal commitment by writing a "promise to yourself." This is a simple but powerful way to reaffirm your intentions for maintaining your sense of peace and renewal. Your promise could be as straightforward as committing to a weekly moment of self-care or practicing gratitude every morning.

Write it down and keep it somewhere accessible, such as in your journal or on your phone. This promise will remind you to stay intentional about your well-being and serve as a motivational tool to help you stay grounded and balanced as you return to your everyday life.

Sunrise to Sunset:

Anchoring Your Day with Purpose

As you wrap up your time by the beach and prepare to return to the rhythm of daily life, it's helpful to carry the calm and joy of your beach retreat with you. One of the most effective ways to do this is by beginning and ending each day with intention. This practice anchors you in moments of peace, mindfulness, and gratitude, helping you face life's demands with clarity and calm. By setting a positive tone at the start and closing your day with reflection, you can carry that sense of serenity forward into your routine, no matter where you are.

To start your day with intention, take a quiet moment when you first wake up. Before you dive into the hustle and bustle, pause to connect with your breath and the present moment. You might think of one or two things you're grateful for—whether it's the warmth of the sun, the comfort of your bed, or the simple joy of a new day. Allow this feeling of gratitude to set the tone for the day ahead, giving you a clear, grounded start. Whether you practice deep breathing or just listen to the sounds around you, taking time for this peaceful pause will help you approach your day with a sense of calm and openness.

Creating this intentional start to your day doesn't have to be a complex ritual. It can be as simple as savoring your morning coffee while watching the waves roll in or taking a moment to enjoy the gentle sounds of nature. Even a short walk or stretching by the water can ground you in the present and remind you to connect with the world around you. Whatever it is, choose something that brings you joy and helps you center your thoughts. This will set the stage for the rest of your day, allowing you to navigate the world with a heart full of gratitude and a mind at ease.

As the day winds down, take a few moments to reflect on what you've experienced. Whether you spend your evening journaling or simply sitting quietly, use this time to process your day with intention. Think about the moments that made you smile, the connections you've had, and the things you're thankful for. Let go of any stress or tension, and allow yourself to relax into a peaceful state of mind before you drift off to sleep. This practice of unwinding with gratitude reinforces a sense of calm and fulfillment, ensuring that you close your day with a peaceful heart.

The beauty of starting and ending your day with intention lies in its simplicity. By taking a few mindful moments to reflect, breathe, and appreciate, you carry the peaceful energy of your time by the ocean into every part of your routine. These practices create a grounding rhythm that helps you stay centered and joyful, no matter how busy life becomes. Over time, these small rituals will become a natural part of your day, cultivating a lasting sense of well-being and balance, no matter where your journey takes you.

Sand and Sea:

A Tangible Reminder of Your Reset

One of the most powerful ways to carry forward the peace and joy you've experienced during a retreat or restful time is by creating a small, tangible reminder of that reset. This memento, whether it's a shell, a photograph, or a small object from nature, can serve as a physical representation of the calm and renewal you've cultivated.

By creating a token of your reset, you are giving yourself a constant source of inspiration that will remind you of the intentional peace you've found and help you reconnect with those feelings when life gets busy or stressful.

The process of choosing or creating a token begins with reflection. As you prepare to leave your retreat or reset experience, take a moment to reflect on the moments that brought you peace, joy, or a sense of renewal. Perhaps you experienced a quiet moment by the ocean, found tranquility in a forest, or enjoyed a beautiful sunset. Select an object that captures the essence of that experience.

For example, you might pick up a smooth shell from the beach, collect a beautiful leaf, or take a photograph of a peaceful scene. The important part is that the object holds meaning for you and represents the stillness and joy you want to carry with you.

Once you've selected your token, find a special place for it. This could be somewhere in your home or workspace where you'll see it often. Each time you encounter the object, let it serve as a reminder of the calm and peace you've experienced.

You might choose to hold the token in your hand when you're feeling stressed, take a moment to reflect on its meaning, and reconnect with the feelings of tranquility it represents. The token becomes a symbol of your reset, a way to anchor yourself in positive emotions and stay grounded when life feels overwhelming.

In addition to its personal meaning, a token can also act as a prompt for self-care and mindfulness. Whenever you notice the object, use it as an opportunity to pause, take a deep breath, and focus on the present moment. Let

Living the Tide:

Infusing Everyday Life with Beachside Serenity

A "beach mindset" is more than just a vacation state of mind—it's a conscious approach to life that prioritizes calm, presence, and joy. To carry the benefits of your retreat into daily life, it's essential to set an intentional habit that reflects the simplicity and peace you experienced. Whether it's a morning ritual, a mindful pause, or an evening reflection, this habit becomes your way of staying connected to the clarity and renewal of your time away. With small, consistent practices, you can transform the fleeting feelings of retreat into lasting emotional balance and resilience.

The first step in creating your "beach mindset" habit is identifying a practice that resonated with you during your time away. Think about the activities that brought you the most peace—perhaps it was walking by the water, journaling your thoughts, or simply sitting quietly and enjoying the scenery. Consider how this activity made you feel and how you can adapt it to your everyday routine. For example, if you found joy in sunrise walks along the shore, you might schedule a quiet morning walk in your neighborhood or local park. The key is to translate the essence of the activity into something accessible and sustainable for daily life.

Once you've chosen your habit, commit to incorporating it into your routine. Start small by designating a specific time and place to practice it. For instance, you might spend five minutes each morning focusing on gratitude or take a mindful pause at lunchtime to reconnect with your breath. Keep the habit simple and manageable to ensure it fits seamlessly into your day. Consistency is crucial; even a brief moment of calm can have a profound impact when practiced regularly. By making this habit part of your routine, you create a touchpoint that reminds you to slow down and savor the present, no matter how busy life gets.

Another way to strengthen your "beach mindset" habit is by pairing it with a positive intention. Before starting your practice, take a moment to reflect on why you're doing it. Are you seeking more calm, focus, or joy in your day? By aligning your habit with a specific intention, you give it purpose and meaning. This helps you stay motivated and ensures the practice feels rewarding, even on hectic days. Over time, this habit will become a natural part of your routine, providing a steady source of peace and grounding amidst life's challenges.

A "beach mindset" habit is a powerful tool for maintaining the balance and joy you experienced during your retreat. By choosing an activity that resonates with you, committing to it consistently, and aligning it with a positive intention, you create a lasting connection to the peace and renewal of your time away. This habit becomes a daily reminder of your ability to find calm and joy, no matter where you are or what challenges you face. With practice, it can transform not just your routine but your overall outlook on life.

Lines in the Sand:

A Written Commitment to Your Peace

Writing a personal promise to yourself can solidify the mindset and positive habits you've developed during your retreat. This simple yet profound exercise helps you affirm your commitment to maintaining peace, gratitude, and mindfulness in your everyday life. By putting your intentions into words, you create a tangible reminder of your goals and the meaningful progress you've made.

Begin by finding a quiet, comfortable space where you can reflect without distractions. Take a few deep breaths to ground yourself in the present moment. Think about the experiences that brought you peace and clarity throughout your retreat. What habits or insights resonated with you the most? Use these reflections as the foundation for your promise. Write from the heart, focusing on how you intend to carry these lessons forward.

Your promise doesn't need to be lengthy or elaborate; simplicity is key. For example, you might write, "I promise to start each day with gratitude and approach challenges with patience." Or, "I commit to taking time for myself each week to reconnect with peace and joy." The act of writing helps reinforce your intentions and provides a powerful touchstone to return to when life becomes busy or stressful.

Keep your written promise in a place where you'll see it regularly, such as a journal, on your desk, or by your bedside. Seeing it often will remind you of your commitment and help you stay aligned with your refreshed mindset. Over time, this promise becomes a source of encouragement, guiding you back to the calm and centeredness you've cultivated.

This exercise is not about perfection but about progress. There will be days when maintaining your promise feels challenging, and that's okay. Use those moments as opportunities to revisit your words and recommit to your goals. Remember, this promise is a tool to help you navigate life with greater resilience and mindfulness.

Ocean-Born Serenity:

Carrying the Calm Back with You

The end of a retreat is not simply a departure; it is a transition into a renewed way of living. The experiences of joy, peace, and mindfulness gained during the retreat are not meant to stay behind but to travel with you as tools for daily life. By consciously carrying forward the lessons and practices learned, you can create a lasting sense of calm and intention in your everyday routine.

One of the most effective ways to maintain this transformation is through mindful habits. Practices such as taking daily moments of gratitude, continuing a "beach mindset" activity like quiet reflection, or engaging with physical reminders, such as a small token, can reinforce your renewed perspective. These rituals become touchstones for anchoring yourself to the peace you discovered, especially when life feels chaotic or overwhelming.

Incorporating intentional transitions like "bliss bookends" can further strengthen this sense of calm. Starting the day with joy and mindfulness and ending it with reflection creates a rhythm of peace that frames your days with purpose. These moments remind you that calm is a choice that can be cultivated, regardless of external circumstances.

Another essential element of bringing the calm home is connection. Sharing your experiences with loved ones and encouraging them to explore similar practices can help deepen the lessons of your retreat. By fostering a supportive environment where mindfulness and joy are shared, you amplify the benefits for yourself and others. Connection also reinforces the intention to sustain the inner peace you've worked to cultivate.

Finally, carry forward the commitment to self-care. Promising yourself that you'll prioritize mindfulness, gratitude, and balance ensures that the retreat doesn't just remain a temporary escape but becomes a foundation for living intentionally. This promise is a declaration that your well-being is worth investing in, and that peace and joy are not luxuries but necessities.

Waves of Renewal:

Bringing Beach Vibes to Your World

The practices developed during a retreat—whether creating a meaningful token, setting new habits, or writing a promise to oneself—serve as powerful tools for sustaining a peaceful mindset. These intentional acts not only mark the culmination of a transformative week but also provide a foundation for navigating the stresses of everyday life with greater ease. By reflecting on these practices and integrating them into daily routines, it becomes possible to maintain the sense of calm and joy cultivated during the retreat.

One key takeaway is the value of creating a physical token that serves as a reminder of the peace you experienced. Whether it's a shell, a photograph, or a small memento, this object can anchor you to the feelings of gratitude and clarity that the retreat fostered. Keeping this token in a visible or meaningful place ensures it acts as a visual cue, helping you reconnect with those positive emotions even amidst life's challenges.

Equally important is the establishment of new habits inspired by the retreat's "beach mindset." Simple actions like taking morning walks, practicing mindfulness with your coffee, or setting aside time for quiet reflection create a daily rhythm of peace and balance. These habits act as touch points throughout the day, reminding you that joy and mindfulness are within reach. When practiced consistently, they can transform how you approach even the most hectic days.

The promise you made to yourself during the retreat solidifies your commitment to prioritizing calm and mindfulness. Whether written as a letter or a short statement, this promise is a personal reminder of your intention to maintain balance in your life. Returning to it during difficult moments can help ground you, reaffirming your ability to choose peace and clarity over stress.

Ultimately, these practices are tools for a joyful, less stressful life. Life's challenges are inevitable, but the lessons learned during the retreat show that calmness is always an option. By revisiting these practices and embracing the intention behind them, you can stay grounded and carry the retreat's peaceful mindset into every aspect of your routine.

Anchored in Renewal: Embracing Your Fresh Start

As you close this chapter of your journey, it's important to take a moment and celebrate the work you've done in using your beach vacation as a true reset for your mind, body, and spirit. What began as a simple getaway has transformed into a powerful opportunity for self-reflection and growth. You've taken the time to immerse yourself in the present, away from the noise and stress of daily life, and in doing so, you've cultivated a deeper sense of peace and clarity. This reset was not just about escaping; it was about reconnecting—with yourself, your values, and the world around you.

Throughout this journey, you've practiced mindfulness, intentionality, and gratitude—each action contributing to the transformation of how you experience the world. Whether it was through creating meaningful rituals, cultivating new habits, or simply pausing to reflect, every step you've taken has brought you closer to a life centered in calmness and joy. The tools and practices you've incorporated into your life during this reset, such as your "beach mindset" habit and meaningful mementos, will continue to be sources of grounding and peace in your everyday routines.

One of the most important lessons you've learned is the power of presence. By being fully present in the moment, you've discovered that true peace comes from slowing down, savoring what's around you, and letting go of the distractions that often pull you away from what truly matters.

This isn't a lesson confined to the beach—it's a mindset that can be brought into your everyday life, whether you're sipping your morning coffee, taking a walk, or simply pausing to breathe. The calmness you've experienced on this journey is something you can carry forward and integrate into all areas of your life.

As you move beyond this retreat, the real work begins. You've gained the insight, clarity, and tools to maintain this sense of peace, and now it's about putting it into practice. Life will continue to present its challenges, but you now have the tools to approach those moments with a fresh perspective—one that's rooted in mindfulness, intention, and joy. Whether through simple daily rituals or deeper reflections, you can continue to nurture the peace you've discovered and carry it with you wherever you go.

Ultimately, this journey wasn't just about your time away—it's about how you choose to live every day with intention and balance. As you step back into your routine, carry forward the lessons of the beach, the peace you've cultivated, and the joy that comes from a life lived mindfully. Your reset has equipped you with the tools to navigate both the calm and the challenges of life with resilience, and that is something truly worth celebrating. Keep your commitment to peace and self-care alive, and let this reset be the beginning of a new, fulfilling way of living.

Waves of Change:

Infusing Your Days with Ocean Calm

As you prepare to return from your beach vacation, the true value of your reset lies in how you carry forward the lessons learned during your time away. The calm, clarity, and mindfulness you experienced on the beach are not meant to be temporary. Instead, these practices can become powerful tools to help you navigate the busyness and stress of everyday life. Here are some practical tips to ensure that the peace and renewal you gained during your vacation continue to influence your routine and mindset moving forward.

One of the most important lessons from your beach reset is the power of slowing down. Life often feels rushed, but the beach taught you the importance of pausing and appreciating the present moment. To apply this in your daily life, start by carving out time each day to slow down—whether it's through a few minutes of mindful breathing, a quiet cup of coffee, or simply pausing to take in your surroundings. These moments of stillness help to recharge your energy and remind you that peace is always available if you take the time to access it.

Another key takeaway from your retreat is the importance of creating a calming environment. Just as the beach provides a peaceful space for reflection and relaxation, you can replicate this in your daily life by cultivating areas in your home or workspace that promote serenity. Whether it's adding plants, lighting candles, or simply clearing clutter, creating a space that fosters calm will help you reconnect to the peace you felt on vacation, even amidst daily demands.

Consider the practice of gratitude, which likely enhanced your sense of joy and presence while at the beach. Bringing this practice home can be transformative. Begin and end each day by reflecting on things you're grateful for. This simple habit can shift your focus away from stress and frustration, helping you to stay grounded and appreciative of life's simple pleasures. Gratitude helps to foster a positive mindset, reducing negative thoughts and promoting emotional well-being.

Incorporating movement into your routine is another valuable lesson from your beach reset. Whether it was walking along the shore or stretching in the sand, physical movement can boost your mood and energy. To carry this lesson forward, aim to incorporate some form of movement into your daily routine, whether it's a morning walk, yoga, or just stretching during breaks. Regular movement not only benefits your body but also enhances your mental clarity and emotional health.

Finally, remember the importance of connection, both to yourself and others. Your beach vacation likely gave you the space to reflect and reconnect with your inner self, and perhaps also to bond with others. Back in everyday life, make time for meaningful connections—whether it's spending quality time with loved ones, reaching out to friends, or simply taking time to check in with your own feelings. Connecting with others and yourself fosters a sense of belonging and emotional well-being, which is crucial for maintaining the peace you cultivated during your vacation.

All of the lessons you've learned on your beach retreat can be life-changing if you continue to apply them daily. By creating moments of stillness, cultivating peaceful spaces, practicing gratitude, staying physically active, and nurturing connections, you can carry the serenity and joy of your vacation into your everyday life. The practices you've developed over the course of your retreat are not just for a limited time—they are tools that will help you find balance, resilience, and happiness long after the sand has settled.

Sunset Breezes:

Ending the Day with a Sunset Meditation

As the sun dips below the horizon, casting golden and coral hues across the water, we are reminded of the importance of closure. Just as the day has its natural rhythm of beginning and ending, so too do the chapters in our lives. Taking time to pause and reflect as the day comes to an end allows us to release the tension we may have gathered and embrace the peace that follows.

The beach, with its rhythmic waves and vast open skies, is a perfect place to cultivate this practice. Its beauty reminds us that every ending holds the promise of renewal. Just as the tides ebb and flow, the setting sun whispers that tomorrow is a fresh opportunity to begin again.

Bringing each day to a meaningful end can be transformative. It is a chance to let go of the unfinished tasks and unanswered questions, to quiet the mental chatter, and to reconnect with the present moment. A sunset meditation invites you to savor the day's gifts, no matter how small, and to drift into rest with a heart full of gratitude and ease.

As you sit on the sand, feeling the cool breeze and hearing the gentle crash of the waves, allow yourself to be fully present. This is your time to reflect, to breathe deeply, and to simply be.

Sunset Meditation

1. Find Your Spot
Settle into a comfortable spot where you can see the horizon. Feel the coolness of the sand beneath you and notice the gentle rhythm of the waves. Take a moment to adjust your posture, sitting tall yet relaxed, your hands resting on your knees or in your lap.

2. Connect with Your Breath
Close your eyes or keep them softly focused on the horizon. Begin to take slow, deep breaths in through your nose and out through

your mouth. Feel your body relax with each exhale, as if you are releasing the day's tensions into the waves.

3. Reflect on the Day

As you watch the sun begin its descent, bring to mind the moments of the day that brought you joy or a sense of accomplishment. Let these memories fill you with warmth, like the last golden rays of sunlight.

4. Release What No Longer Serves You

Picture the waves carrying away any worries or unresolved thoughts from the day. With each exhale, imagine these concerns dissolving into the ocean, leaving you lighter and more at peace.

5. Embrace the Present Moment

Turn your focus to the beauty around you—the colors of the sky, the sound of the water, the feel of the breeze. Let yourself be completely present, soaking in the serenity of this moment.

6. Set an Intention for Tomorrow

As the last sliver of the sun disappears, take a moment to set a gentle intention for the coming day. Perhaps it's to approach the day with gratitude, kindness, or curiosity.

7. Close with Gratitude

Finish by expressing gratitude—for the day, the sunset, the ocean, and this moment of peace. When you feel ready, slowly open your eyes and take in your surroundings before making your way back.

Hearts of Light:

Carrying the Sunset Within

As the final colors of the sunset fade into twilight, you may feel a sense of calm and renewal washing over you. This moment of peace, carved out just for you, is more than a vacation ritual; it's a practice of connection and self-care that you can carry home with you.

The beach teaches us valuable lessons about the rhythm of life—of beginnings and endings, of release and renewal. By dedicating time to reflect and let go each evening, you're not just witnessing the sunset but embodying its wisdom. It's a simple yet profound way to honor the day that's passed and prepare your mind and heart for the day ahead.

When you return home, you might not have the sound of waves or the salty breeze, but the essence of this meditation remains within you. A sunset can be experienced in many forms—a quiet moment at your window, a walk through your neighborhood as the sky darkens, or even a few breaths of gratitude before bed.

These moments are your anchor, a way to ground yourself amidst the busyness of life.

As you continue your journey, let the practice of ending each day with intention remind you of your time at the beach. Just as the ocean tides remain constant no matter where you are, so too can your commitment to inner peace and reflection.

Take this ritual with you, and let it be a small but powerful part of your life, bringing you back to yourself no matter where you may roam.

Conclusion ~

A Fond Farewell

A Return to Self:

Drawing Endless Strength from the Sea

As you return to your daily life, remember that the lessons you gained from the beach are not meant to fade with the passing days. The ocean, with its rhythm and timeless presence, offers a wellspring of wisdom that can guide you through life's most challenging moments. Whenever you feel overwhelmed or disconnected from the peace you cultivated during your retreat, take a moment to reconnect with the lessons of the sea. The ocean teaches us patience, resilience, and the power of being fully present, lessons that are invaluable when life becomes hectic.

The first piece of wisdom the ocean offers is the importance of flow. Just as the tide moves in and out, life ebbs and flows, with moments of calm and moments of turbulence. When you face stress, remember that, like the ocean, you too can find your rhythm amidst the chaos.

Allow yourself to move with the flow of life, knowing that difficult moments will pass, and stillness will return. In times of uncertainty or overwhelm, take a deep breath and let the current of your thoughts and emotions subside, just as the waves recede.

Another valuable lesson from the ocean is the power of renewal. The ocean's waves continuously crash upon the shore, only to retreat and come back again - reminding us that each moment is an opportunity for renewal.

When life feels like it's weighing you down, you can use the ocean's energy to refresh your mindset. Think of each wave as a symbol of new beginnings and growth. Allow yourself to reset, release tension, and emerge from difficult moments feeling renewed, just as the sea constantly renews itself with each tide.

The ocean also reminds us of the power of stillness. Though the waves may crash energetically against the shore, beneath the surface, the water remains still and peaceful. This calm beneath the surface is a metaphor for the quiet center within you, even in the midst of life's challenges.

When you feel overwhelmed, take a moment to breathe deeply, grounding yourself in the stillness that exists within. Like the ocean, you too have the ability to remain calm and centered, even when the surface of your life is turbulent.

Additionally, the ocean's vastness reminds us of the importance of perspective. When faced with overwhelming situations, it's easy to get caught in the small details. The ocean, vast and expansive, encourages us to step back and gain perspective on our challenges.

Just as the horizon stretches out endlessly, so too can our sense of possibility. Remember that what seems overwhelming in the moment may be part of a larger, unfolding story. By taking a step back, we allow ourselves to view situations from a calmer, clearer standpoint.

In conclusion, the ocean's wisdom is always available to you, especially during times when life feels overwhelming. By remembering the flow, renewal, stillness, and perspective that the sea offers, you can find your way back to the peace and balance you cultivated during your retreat.

The ocean teaches us that no matter how stormy life may seem, calmness is always within reach. Keep the ocean's wisdom close, and let it guide you through life's challenges, helping you to stay grounded, resilient, and at peace.

Sea Breezes of Balance:

Embracing Peace, No Matter Where You Are

As you reach the end of this journey, it's important to reflect on the profound lessons the beach has shared with you. The time spent in a peaceful, reset environment has equipped you with tools to navigate the complexities of life with a renewed sense of clarity and calm. You've learned that rest and reflection are powerful forces that can shift your mindset and open you up to more peaceful, intentional living.

These lessons are not confined to the shore—they are accessible to you at any moment, wherever you are. Life may become busy or overwhelming again, but the peace you've cultivated can stay with you if you continue to nurture it.

One of the most valuable gifts from your beach reset is the understanding that renewal is not a one-time event, but an ongoing process. Just like the ocean that continually renews itself with every wave, you too have the ability to reset at any time.

The tools and practices you've discovered—whether through mindful habits, grounding techniques, or simple moments of gratitude—are your reminders that peace is always available. The ebb and flow of your thoughts, emotions, and life circumstances are natural, but with intentional practices, you can always return to a state of calm, no matter what comes your way.

Renewal doesn't require a specific place or external conditions; it's an inner state you can tap into wherever you are. The habits you've formed—taking moments to breathe deeply, reflecting on your intentions, or practicing mindfulness—can become a part of your daily routine.

These small but powerful acts of self-care act as anchors, helping you to stay grounded and centered no matter where you are. Just as the beach taught you to embrace the present moment and let go of worries, you can carry that same awareness with you into the everyday rhythms of your life.

Remember, peace is not something you have to search for outside yourself. It's always within reach, no matter your environment. You've already experienced it during your retreat, and now you have the ability to access it at any time. By making space for moments of quiet reflection, being intentional with your thoughts and actions, and honoring your needs, you create a life that reflects peace, clarity, and joy. Life may throw challenges your way, but with the practices you've cultivated, you'll always have the tools to return to a place of balance and inner calm.

Always know in your heart that the power of renewal is always available to you. It's not tied to a vacation, a specific place, or a particular moment—it's an ongoing process that you can carry with you. The peace, clarity, and joy you've discovered are not just fleeting feelings; they are part of who you are.

So, as you move forward, remember that the ocean's wisdom is always within you, and with every new day, you have the opportunity to renew, to find peace, and to live with intention. Embrace this power of renewal, and let it guide you toward a life filled with calm, purpose, and a deep sense of peace wherever you are.

Acknowledgments

This book would not have been possible without the love, encouragement, and inspiration of so many. To my family and friends, thank you for your unwavering belief in me. To Frank, Helga, Tim, Lisa, Jacky, and Steve, thank you for providing a precious sanctuary in which to live and write.

To my Reighanna, your guidance and feedback shaped this work into something I am truly proud of.

A special thanks to the families who entrusted me with the care of their homes and beloved pets. Your kindness and generosity provided me with peaceful spaces to reflect, write, and create.

To Calvin, Leeloo, Slater, Tyler, Davis, Sam, Winston, Whitey, Precious, Goldie, Sweet Pea, Finnley, Bailey, Sammy, Sophie, Yinny, Milo, Marley, Sugar, Spice, Shadow, Selah, Boo Boy, Tickety, Duff, Paris, Koko, Winne, Hunny, Hobie, Little Dude, Duke, Kai, Ginger, Luna, Roxie, Maverick, Buzz, Sandy, Tuke, Melody, Bocelli, Lux, Lemon, Luna and Stormy—thank you for your quiet companionship, playful energy, and the joy you brought to this journey.

To the readers, may this book bring you the peace and renewal you seek. And finally, to the beaches of Brunswick County, for being a constant source of calm, inspiration, and healing.

Sandy Hugs and Salty Kisses,
Caroline